The Power of the Holy Spirit

Come O Holy Spirit

—— by ——

J A Russell

authorHOUSE®

AuthorHouse™ UK
1663 Liberty Drive
Bloomington, IN 47403 USA
www.authorhouse.co.uk
Phone: 0800.197.4150

Scripture quotations marked NJB are from The New Jerusalem Bible, copyright © 1985 by Darton, Longman
& Todd, Ltd. and Doubleday, a division of Random House, Inc. Reprinted by Permission.

Published by AuthorHouse 07/02/2015

ISBN: 978-1-5049-3996-6 (sc)
ISBN: 978-1-5049-3997-3 (e)

Print information available on the last page.

Any people depicted in stock imagery provided by Thinkstock are models,
and such images are being used for illustrative purposes only.
Certain stock imagery © Thinkstock.

This book is printed on acid-free paper.

We can know that we are living in Him
and He is living in us
because He lets us share His Spirit.
1 Jn.4:13

The Power of The Holy Spirit

Come O Holy Spirit

Seasons of the Soul
Christian Prose and Poetry
by J A Russell

'I Am Who I Am.

This is My name for all time;
by this name I shall be invoked for all generations to come.'
Ex.3:15

The Alpha and The Omega

The Beginning and the End

Contents

Hope

Hope is the flame that must burn always.
If allowed to dim or flicker
the fight can be lost and gone for ever

Hope is the driving force that embraces anxiety

Hope must not come to an end.
It must be bright and constant as the rising of the sun
and even if sometimes clouded over
it is always there glowing strong and solid
certain that the mist will be put aside

If Hope dies, life dies
and withers away like a youthful plant knew its prime
and in due season produced wondrous fruits,
but now all hopes of gentle rains have gone.
The branches turn limp;
the once upright yet supple stem
which allowed such beautiful play
and showed such graceful dancing to the wind
becomes brittle, no more ready to sway at its friendly touch.
But rather would it snap and be forgetful of itself
and all it once knew.
Despair. Defeat. Discouragement. Dark

Hope is Light

Hope is forever knowing we are tended by a Master Gardener
who sends refreshing springs
to quench our thirst
who gives gentle dews
so soft we fail to notice

Hope is the beyond which lives today

Peace

Peace is like the stillness after war
following the raging of battle
when survivors stare thankfully around
at the starkness of death
in the lonely silence which can be felt
but to which no man would gladly offer his hand

Peace is like a bird nesting in its home;
so strong the winds that near broke his fragile wings
now gladly folded in the smell and heat
of the waste and remnants that became his fortress
that offers shelter till the storm subsides

Like a baby slumbering on its mothers breast
feeding in the warmth of her body
undisturbed and unaware of all else
as one in her embrace

Like a flower standing upright
after squally showers almost forced the last breath
from its drooping branches

Like a ship knows harbour, glad to be once again resting
in the familiar and secure place
that always lent safety before another voyage
with fond surroundings and friendships everlasting

Like the utter tranquillity of a lake
held in the firmness of the hands of cupped mountains
knowing its place, glad to be there
protected by these guardians
who can but compliment each other
in their beauty and serenity

Peace is in the silence of the sun
as it breaks through the skies
to herald the arrival of a new day
unbroken as the movement of the earth itself

Also that which follows anguish
in bringing new life into this world
that moment of relief when all is well
and worries all unfounded
that uncapturable moment
the unforgettable climax of life born anew

Peace is as unseen as the breath
that supports the very heavens
unheard in its comings and goings
knowing no limits to its strength in all it upholds

Peace as the body now lies
exhausted by frustration and fear.
Freed from the flesh that became its prison.
Free to roam without itself
unhindered
by the weight it seems to have borne forever.
Freed from its torturer, cruel pain,
tormented by memories it once knew
of carefree movements
that came as easily as the flowing of the tide
now a lifeless form
glad to leave behind all that wearied it so.
Could one deny such comfort
though we must wait to share this release.
Yet rather rejoice in God's will

Peace, true Peace, is that Gift imparted
to the soul belonging only to Christ
the richest Gift bequeathed by Him
a part of Heaven on this earth, some share of Him even now
that brings Eternal Light to His beloved ones

Jesus said, 'Peace I bequeath to you.
My own Peace I give you,
a Peace the world cannot give, this is My gift to you.' Jn.14:27

The Chalice of Life

The Chalice is made of gold so pure
it can contain all it is offered, all that is poured into it
because it is of gold and is incorruptible and will know no tarnish.
Even as gold it must first be smelted under
the burning flames of the furnace, ground down and refined
leaving no impurity within lest it fail proven.
Then it needs know the loving hands
which carefully goad its mindful shape and purpose
totally trusting the tenderness
yet force inflicted by the weight of the bludgeon
for its kindness in making it as smooth as the lining of a silken sky

It is done. It is complete. Yet it is empty,
a thing cast aside which knows no purpose
if not to be raised to offer drink to serve another

There must be that day when the first drops of precious wine
fit only for the purest vessel
will meet the inner cup splashing upon its virginal emptiness
both rejoicing with equal delight, to now be purposeful
one useless unless it touches the other
for what use is emptiness if not to be filled
what value good wine if not to be tasted

So begins the true life of giving and receiving
the mystery of emptiness yet fullness
till all at once it is transformed, all so unseen and unsought
finding itself held so tenderly within the firm hands of its Creator
who once lent such harsh treatment
now seeing the goodness that if a cup is empty
so it can be filled

The deeper the hollow the fuller with wine
till it flows in abundance from its endless source
breaking into tiny streams that bid all to taste
and delight in its eternal goodness

Who But God

Who but God can measure the emptying of heart
and know when to give
fullness of grace

Love

Love is total giving just as a mother gives her body giving birth
to be used to bring forth another soul for its Creator
to be the vessel which sets it forth on its journey
for even in this new day comes also the returning back
to God all He so freely lends

Love stands silent as a sentinel over young loves
guarding their self-images
desiring for them to share the same Love
desiring they travel the Way of their accord
and seek the Peace that offers rest and consolation.
Though Love stands in silence it shows by 'being' and
grants the freedom to learn which causes pain to Love

Love is equal in the differences it brings
Love is looking deep within, not without,
to where lies all the beauty that tells its tale to its beholder.
Here can be learnt the willingness of Love
the unwavering force that promises to go on, to give oneself
over to the unknown with each new day that dawns.
Here lies all the past that alone can tell the wounds and scars
of sad old yesterday
the hopes that faded with maturity
the tears that moulded it to now
the pain and disappointments of reality

Love is ever giving for true joy is found in this wonder

Love is God in action. Love is God on earth
Love is God manifest on the Cross
showing Love
Love eternal, Love unconditional,
for all mankind. Amen

'I shall give you a new heart, and put a new spirit in you;
I shall remove the heart of stone from your bodies
and give you a heart of flesh instead.' Ez.36:26-27

Prayer Is a Step

Prayer is a step to a Loving God that can never be taken away
Nothing on earth, not even death, can diminish God as we pray

Prayer is a step on which to stand on the stairwell to God Whom we meet
Nothing and no one, no power, no words, can take it from under our feet

Prayer is strength from the Holy Spirit dwelling in hearts from above
Forever upheld by His Holy arm, constantly shielded by Love

Prayer is a platform for speaking to God where He hears all the soul has to say
Hopes may be dashed, still His Presence remains and shall never be taken away

God is ready to hear. He knows our needs, how sorely we seek His attention
Prayer, that place to never move from, lets His hand show Divine intervention

God gave us this gift, our right to be heard, on the Cross that terrible day
For He gave His Son who gave Himself. Light that cannot be stolen away

Prayer is a step on which to stand as we patiently wait a reply
From God who shows this comes from Him, through the Son who came to die

Prayer is a hold we can have on God for He promised to guide the way
He delights in us, as we in Him, providing we don't turn away

Prayer is a two-way conversation, a dialogue, one to one
With a Loving Father, who in the Spirit, answers us through the Son

The Cross is that spot on which to stand, the place that joined Heaven to earth
Linking our prayers to the Trinity, bringing grace and new birth

Joy

Joy is the eternal well of happiness
flowing freely from within
which sweeps away
the weariness and worries of a laboured day
bringing along contentment
and thankfulness that again
there is refreshment for tomorrow
in the gathering of today

Each day is a learning of tomorrow
building upon the root of knowledge
stored for all time, ready for use and action

Without today we would not know
how to greet tomorrow, neither tears nor laughter.
There is certainty in the uncertainty of tomorrow
for the heart could not today
bear all the tellings of the future

Joy can be silent
ringing out not in hollow echoes
but with gentleness
that in flowing to another
brings holiness and calm
and even seeing all swept briskly aside
knows all will turn to good with steadfastness
because it is yet another learning
another experience to enrich life

And Joy is found in knowing more of self

Children

O What bringers of wisdom are these little shoots!

They teach most all we know in matters of the heart and of self
They reveal patience or lack of it
They test its resources and always want for more

They need time, for how careless would it be in accepting
Such a jewel not to cherish it
Happy the child who is nourished by warmth and true affection
Rather than rich clothing and worldly rewards
Time was so freely given, time we must freely return

In their searching and seeking
The spade of our intellect digs deep within our bed of earth
To rediscover so much buried wisdom

They have the freedom of the young
To tread over the paths of our minds and hearts

What blessings we gather from them
What joys they hand us with their smiles
What sadness they hand us with their tears
What pride, wonder, pain, they give us with their growth
Yet freely came my roots, so too will theirs be given

Freedom is found only in truth
And if someday the most beauteous blossom of all
Is desired by the Master Gardener
To enhance a distant field, to grace another garden
Or chosen to be His own delight
This is to be our joy in knowing so

The Advocate

The Word that transforms and renews life
The Word that gives insight and learning to the simple
The Word that melts the heart of steel
The Word that shames the bold and encourages the weak
That feeds the hungry and lights the darkness
Speaks in silence and humbles the proud
Warms the chill and calms the storm, stills the wagging tongue
And breaks down the strongest barrier man erects

The Word gives an infinite store of knowledge
To the libraries of our mind
This greatest Informer lives within a heart so pure
It leads to all Truth

Truth is like an island
That stands above the restless waters it shares with waves
That whisper different sounds in their shifting
Rather as the sun is unaffected
With the changes of the seasons it produces by being

Truth touches something profound as it fills the expectant space
That now becomes a Living Word
Responsive and reliable as it forces out all else but Truth.
In listening growth increases
Joyous in discovering as to be found
Flowing from an endless well of knowledge
Rather as clouds float across the sky revealing themselves
But ever making way for newer shapes generous in their task

Just as a pen knows the limits of its writer so we can limit God

The Countenance of Christ

The Living Countenance of Christ
God plants within a soul
To captivate with but a glance
So many words are told

The memory of this Dear Face
Gives certainty of more
Beckoning to follow Him
In faith through every door

The Face of Christ upon the Cross
Tells man all he has done
As if each day He dies anew
Our Father's only Son

The Blessed Countenance of Christ
Reveals the Living God
He shows the mysteries are true
Jesus, Flesh and Blood

As God Divine, the Risen Lord
The Father in the Son
The Spirit's Dove, the Trinity
Blessed Three in One

Each person can discover Him
The Lord, that hiding place
To thank Him He so blesses us
With the Countenance of His Face

My heart has said of You, 'Seek His face.'
Yahweh, I do seek Your face. Ps.27:8

Evil

Evil is that detracting us from God
That which comes between Creator and created
The barrier which comes in many guises
Cutting off from grace and truth and beauty
Leading from the steepness of the climb
Whispering to take an easy way
Full of emptiness and fleeting promises.
Evil speaks in words that flow too freely from its voice
Gushing out unpondered thoughts
Afraid of the loneliness silence may speak of.
Silence fills the space of empty words
Words that were never meant to be devalued so
For sound is a thing of beauty
For the giver and receiver, flowing gently from the lips
To find its way embedded
In the ear and heart of the listener
Both the richer for this precious token of exchange.
One pure drop can penetrate deeper
Than a torrent
Which sweeps aside all, leaving only destruction
But the world is full of volume
Drowning out the One true voice

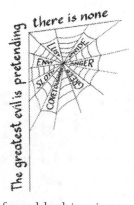

Evil can be found lurking in contentment
Luring us to settle where we are instead of carrying on.
In our stillness we must never settle
For there is nothing to be gained by losing valuable time
That offers more than we could hold
To become as undesirable as stagnant waters

Evil thrives on greed
Laughing at the one who seeks an earthly fortune
Mockingly he claps his hands, cajoling further into his den

The very weight of gold ties man down with all he amasses
The very treasure he seeks becomes his misfortune
The building of his castle draws him from the one true Kingdom
The journey he undertakes but blurs his vision
Wearying him for the real travel of stillness

Yet he who is poor stores riches untold
He who gives away fortunes is blest beyond wealth
He who gives only time
Because it is all he possesses
Gives himself

Of all Evil the greatest is pretending there is none
And once this thought has taken hold all is lost
For this is Evil's proudest moment
And yet - alas for him – his own great stumbling block
In the believer

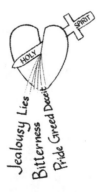

Evil is all that separates man from God
Discreetly weaving in and out of life
Until this thread is snapped in two
By purity of heart
Cutting free
To meet the wide expanse of God
So joined to Him
That nothing comes between
The Beloved and beloved

Death

It's me who's dying this time, can't you see
Come and stay awhile at my side
The cloak of loneliness is over me
I see you. But I'm alone inside

It's me who's dying this time, won't you stay
Come inside and gently close the door
Could you listen as I try to explain
I'm going somewhere I've not gone before

Though I've travelled many miles in my life
This is different. I'm frightened and afraid
It's all so quick. There isn't any time
To put to right some bad mistakes I've made

People say life carries on around me
Why was I born. What was my life about
Won't they stop and bid a friend farewell
Can't they see my time is running out

I'm not prepared. It's much too soon to die
And I know I've offended many friends
If only I could see all of them now
I'd do everything I could to make amends

It's me who's dying this time, can't you see
I just can't seem to make you understand
I am lost. Time is on your side
I need the comfort of a gentle hand

This is me, myself, who is uncertain
A life is ending now and its my own
Can this be really happening to me
It's always been somebody else I've known

It's me who's dying this time, can't you see
Who can I ask to show me what to do
Who knows what happens when we're gone
How would you feel if you were me and I were you

I've heard talk of a man who came to earth
They say He lived though He was murdered I recall
They say He died for me so I may live
Do you think maybe its true after all

Am I a sinner. Me. How did I fail
I carried on and always did my best
I almost worked my fingers to the bone
My body hardly knew a day of rest

Did I question things and try to find the answer
Or take my life for granted until now
Did I take the easy way and never care
Is it too late. Won't someone tell me how

To be thankful for my life though such a trial
Answerable for each hour I've ever spent
To look inside myself. See who I am
I wonder now if this is what they meant

Won't you tell me how to turn and talk to Him
I wish I'd done the things I've seen you do
I've also heard them say He judges us
And want to ask forgiveness if its true

It's me who's dying this time, can't you see
It's possible that this is my last day
Won't you help me now and show me how to die
Will you kneel beside me now. And pray

*He abolished death and He has proclaimed life and immortality
through the Good News. 2 Tm.1:10*

Heaven

Death is the door we shall go through
When we've stepped to the other side
There is only brightness and Light
With no time nor space to divide

We'll meet those who have gone before us
We shall laugh as we laughed before
We shall recognise all our loved ones
When we step through that open door

Think of your happiest moments
The wonderment you have known
Such bliss will last for ever
With grief and sadness flown

All this through the Lord Jesus
Who loved us enough to come
From Heaven to be our Saviour
The Father's only Son

He calls out 'Come and follow'
He gained our eternal home
Our place beside Him always
Gathered around His throne

So we step through this open doorway
This thing we call 'Death' undone
And we take our place in the Kingdom
Through the Victory Jesus won

Let us thank Him and praise Him because
He suffered and died for our sake
Sealing earthly ties with Heavenly Love
Love that can never, never break

How Can I Let Go of You

How can I let go of you
Oh so deep in me
Such parting does not come
easily

How can I let go of you
You were my all
Always there for me. Whatever
should befall

I can't let go. I ache and simply want to be
with you now
My healing is in letting go. But
I don't know how

I just want to wake again and know
your touch, your sound
I can't seem to face the future, without
you around

All the common sense and wisdom
can't take tears away
There is this void no matter what
people say

I can't let go. The pain would worsen,
loss increase
But if I could maybe I'd find
inner peace

When I Am Sad

When I am sad I know that you are smiling
For you have gone. You've entered Heaven's door
I might be sad but you will still be smiling
You're happy now and will be ever more

When I am sad, feeling lost and lonely
I know you'll never feel this way again
For you are gone, living now in Paradise
Released of any suffering or pain

When I am strong, feeling close to Jesus
Who gives me hope and makes Heaven very real
This makes me smile and brings to me some comfort
Knowing this is how you'll ever feel

O thank the Lord He has made it possible
It's His design. He wipes each tear away
In Heaven is only gladness and rejoicing
There to be spared the sorrows of this day

And so I smile to think that you are happy
Happier now than words could ever explain
You are healed, forever in God's Presence
And peace is given praising Jesus name

And as I pray united with the angels
Believing you are free from earthly trial
I can rejoice in God for He has triumphed
Love is your experience all the while

Without a cloud. Never to diminish
Eternal Love that stays surrounding you
Though I shed a tear, I'm glad you now know
The promises Jesus made are true. Amen

To Pain

Knowing Pain taught me how to live
Without this knowledge life was incomplete
Opening my heart creating space
For my Saviour whose Face I yearned to meet

We need a cross to show how weak we are
Pain to see the Way our Saviour trod
We need the sword that opened up His side
And suffering to force us through to God

Such joy in Pain remains a mystery
The ultimate God gives while on this earth
For entering the tomb with Christ reveals
How we die to come know our second birth

Within the precious Cross given to the Son
Lies healing for the body, mind and soul
Through the suffering of Jesus' open wounds
Comes His power to resurrect and make us whole

In knowing Pain life can find its meaning
To drink the Cup of everlasting wine
Embracing the Cross reveals the truth
How Suffering teaches love Divine

What I know now
I have learnt through
suffering

*If we are His children, then we are His heirs, heirs of God and joint-heirs
with Christ, provided we share His sufferings,
so as to share His glory. Rom.8:17*

Unforgiveness

To err is human, to forgive is divine

If I could forgive, I want to know
How would it make me feel
If I forgive, does it make your crime
Any the less real

If I did forgive it might bring regret
My heart be ever more hardened
I might feel even worse than now
By relenting, knowing you're pardoned

If I forgive does it then mean
You'd be better off than me
That I'd be the one imprisoned
And you the one set free

I think of all the damage you've done
My heart still tied up in chains
It is impossible to start afresh
When only bitterness remains

What would I do with the trauma
The darkness that you gave
How can I be rid of this feeling
Shall I carry it to my grave

If I tried to forgive, I want to know
What difference would it make
If I did forgive, though I know I can't
I'd be doing it just for my sake

I'd rather not feel this way but I do
Those happenings can't be denied
Where can I put the anger, the hurt
I'd like to be happy inside

But if I forgave you'd never be sorry
'It's not so bad' you'd recall
So I'll not forgive. We'll both be trapped
And you won't be free after all

Conscience

Is there something I should not have said
Is there something I should have done
Is there something that would have helped
Make things better for everyone

Is there something I should not have done
Is there something I should have said
Is there something that could have made
All things look brighter ahead

Searching around in my soul I'll find
What is best for you and for me
Waiting and praying for Wisdom to speak
Is the secret to harmony

For true Wisdom can never be wrong
Therefore Wisdom can only be right
The perfect way is discovered
By keeping Her ever in sight

Letting Her shine though all actions
Resounding in words we speak
This Gift that down through all ages
Only the bravest seek

Knowing when to speak, when to be quiet
When to act, or when to be still
Learning, seeking, the best thing to do
Discerning God's holy will

Give Your servant a heart to understand
how to discern between good and evil. 1 Kings 3:9-28

Do Not Put Your Light Under a Bushel

We are not meant to be restricted
We are born to thrive and grow
We are born to follow the Spirit
To wherever He may show

We are meant to learn and develop
As we travel through God's land
To take His light and be guided by
The tender touch of His hand

We are born to shine like the stars, to seek all we want to know
We are meant to shine in the darkness as a candle gives its glow

A light is not seen if hidden in a cellar, a cupboard, a room
When locked away it is helpless to scatter away the gloom

God's shining Light is powerful, with healing in its rays
With tenderness and mercy to carry throughout days

Life can be like a picture book, a mixture of joy and dread
Everything held together by the Holy Spirit's thread

Some find life hard and fearful
Where the light of Christ is dim
Sharing our faith is a gift
God gives to shine forth from within

So tell out loud all His wonders
Let the world hear what you might say
For the light shining out in the darkness
Can brighten another's day

Stand on the highest hilltop
If you haven't begun then begin
Giving to God all the glory
For you took your Light from Him!

Free Will

Decide within yourself all you want to do
But let your conscience be one with the Lord
Choose within your heart all you want to be
But let your will meet with Divine accord

Let your aim be for Grace, Wisdom and Truth
And Love flowing from your Father's hand
Search for all that is good. Strive for all that is right
Pray for unending Peace to cover the land

May you call God 'Abba'. May you call Jesus 'Lord'
With the Holy Spirit ever as your Guide
So when He comes upon the clouds, Jesus smiles
As He gathers you tenderly to His side

'Come, thou blessed of My Father'

When the Son of Man comes in His glory,
escorted by all the angels,
then He will take His seat on His throne of glory.
All nations will be assembled before Him
and He will separate people one from another
as the shepherd separates sheep from goats.

He will place the sheep on His right hand and the goats on His left.
Then the King will say to those on His right hand,
'Come, you whom My Father has blessed,
take as your heritage the kingdom prepared for you
since the foundation of the world.' Mt.25:31-34

Within The Veil

Let Him remove the veil
Let Him take aside
All that is delaying you
Let Him make of you His Bride

Let Him take your doubting
Let Him reveal His Love
And gently move the veil to show
How Beauty reigns above

Let Him come and enter
Let His peace prevail
God alone can show you
Let Him remove the veil

The veil is like a blindfold
Shutting all outside
Let Him remove it from you
And take you for His Bride

God is certain that He loves us
You'll have a different view
As the veil is lifted you will see
His gifts prepared for you

Where everything is positive
Showing the other side
When He removes the veil
And you become His Bride

Christ alone can remove it

Their hearts are covered with a veil and this veil will not be taken away
till they turn to the Lord. 2 Cor.3:15

Be Still

Be still. God is found in simplicity
Be still. Hear the silence of Eternity

Be still. God's Presence is around
Be still. An open heart is where He is found

Be still. Not in the mighty wind or fire
But in quiet will you find your heart's desire

Be still. Look to Him. Let His Voice arise
Let Him come and wipe away the tears from your eyes

Be still. God is lost in rushing and in haste
Listen. Love is beckoning you to stop and taste

Be still. Know that God is real
He is with you and He knows the way you feel

'Be still and acknowledge that I am God,
supreme over nations, supreme over the world.' Ps.46:10

Heaven's Ways

When you bang your head against Heaven
With the prayer you know God hears
You may not get all you ask for
Though you wait for many years

When you hang your head in despair
When you knock and seek and call
When it seems God is too busy
And is doing nothing at all

When you cry out loud appealing
In the loneliness of the night
God gives His gentle Presence
To make the darkness bright

When you stand rejected and feel
That God does not understand
No matters how it appears
Our Father has all things in hand

When you ask and search and listen for the Good News of the day
Remember our Father considers how to answer as we pray

For He sees all that is right for us. He sees all that would be wrong
Persistent in His calling to worship Him in song

God loves His royal priesthood. To those He set apart
He gives such special graces, drawing close into His heart

The secret of prayer is to stay
Resting on Heaven's door
Though it might come to us unnoticed
God gives more and more and more

The Father sends all that is good for us
Just as He treated His Son
To bring us nearer His image
And make His Kingdom come

So despite your many questions
And the way that you might feel
God is for ever with us
And God is very real!

The Lamp

I fell into a hole one day
I didn't know how to get out
No one came to rescue me
No matter how hard I'd shout

Then I grew quite despondent
It was uncomfortable and damp
I couldn't find my way around
It was dark. I needed a lamp

And suddenly there without question
The brightest light I'd ever seen
Was standing in front to guide me
I rejoiced! Then thought it a dream

Had it come truly to my assistance
Had it heard my miserable call
There are no steps or stairs or ladders
Oh, there's no way out after all

But this brightest of lights never dimmed
Just beckoned to follow its glow
Where it showed me an open doorway
How it got there I'll never know

I went through the door for I sensed
This light was protecting me
And now the darkness has gone
I'm not stuck in a hole. I am free!

Discernment

Faith

No one need tell another
What is the right thing for them to do
Each person discovers for themselves
All that is perfect and true

No one decides for somebody else
All that their life is about
But you can recommend they listen to God
And at least try to find out

Hope

Encourage each other always
To hear what the Spirit might say
Let Him lead and bless and guide
Expectantly listen and pray

God made us part of His purpose
Each uniquely designed
It is best we try to grasp
All that He has in mind

Charity

We are but part of a jigsaw puzzle
Moving and shifting until
God places us into that perfect spot
Fitting us into His will

For surely God wants us to serve Him
He gives the gifts of His choice
The only way to be certain
Is by waiting upon His Voice

The Mystery

Only if we die can we live. Only if we fail can we rise
Only when we are lost are we found. Only being foolish makes us wise

Only when we are weak do we grow strong
And in grief see the treasure we once knew
In love feel the pain of tenderness
In confusion search for what is true
Only at the ending we begin
When we finish is where we make a start
Only when we have opened can we close
And in stillness feel the moving of the heart

In thirsting is where we drink our fill
In being broken can begin to mend
By forgetting remember all the good
In loneliness discover who is friend
Unity is created by division
As darkness illumes the dimmest star
Despair gives way to perfect hope
In knowing not discover who we are

In silence hear the murmur of the wind
To see it gently resting on a bough
Mother Earth knows the Sender of Her toil
If only man would stop to question 'How?'

Jesus said, 'Unless a wheat grain falls into the earth and dies
it remains only a single grain; but if it dies it yields a rich harvest.' Jn.12:24

God's Holy Mountain

On Your holy mountain Peace
Unceasingly
Undisturbed by storm or trial
Eternally

Beneath the gaze of God
And tender Hand
That fences us within
His holy land

The air we breathe
Renews our life each day
Guiding us by grace
This perfect Way

Our nourishment
The prayer to feed our soul
Replenishing
Always making whole

To eyes so blind
Like orphans we must seem
This life is real and true
Theirs the dream

Come, we will go up to Yahweh's mountain. Micah 4:2

Things To Come

A breath could destroy all He holds
A single breath
that comes from Him to cover earth and all its span
Man underestimates the things in His control and takes for granted
the miracles He performs for us every day
as the earth is sent revolving round the sky
and the moon takes its place to keep its watch at night
and the sun is held as by nothing
and the seasons disappear and reappear continually

What would happen if the sun failed to rise
Or the skies at night were dark as death that knew no end
Or if the earth reversed and swung the other way for a change
Confusion. Disarray. Disbelief

Jesus said, 'The powers of Heaven will be shaken.' Lk.21:-26

If God withdrew the stars and allowed them not
to brighten up the skies, what would man think
If the flowers never opened and the grass never grew and
Spring never came, what would man do
If the rains never came and thirst covered all the land
till it was barren, what could man do
If the sun failed to shine and warm the frozen ground and
gently breathe new life in still earth to grow for man his crops
where would he turn
If God withdrew His love could man survive
Could he endure a time when living or a death
would seem the same. No escape
For living would be to wander aimlessly
and nowhere find comfort from the knowing gaze of God
Dying would be the loss of Paradise so long awaited
If God withdrew His power for just one moment
how man would suffer as the earth drew to a halt
and floods spilt into all he possesses
washing all away but sin

If God withdrew His light such anguish would there be
to never know the timing of the days
when land would turn to waste and deathly cold
would be every turning where we went
If God withdrew His breath that is so faithful
but for a while, earth all would wither
and every adult and every child would stifle gradually
and be no more

So great our God who holds all power and yet
He cares so much for foolish man
He holds the seas and mountains by His fingertips
and watches from beyond the upper skies with sadness
If God gave to man all he deserved how would it be
If He punished him for selfishness and waste and vanity and greed
For arrogance and overwhelming disregard for His authority
For ignorance and blindness to His Son

It would take but one moment for God to show such to man
One tremble of the earth would be enough to make man tumble
from the throne he gave himself

The Humble Poor

The shepherds believed so long ago at Bethlehem
Their simple faith gave them eyes to see the King they now adored
And as in times before the humble poor believe
But did they believe in Jerusalem
The happenings before the Cross
When Jesus said that God was His true Father
Did they believe the message of His healings, His miracles
And that forgiveness is the greatest of them all
Who can forgive but God
They crucified Him for being a blasphemer
Our Saviour who came to earth to bring God's Love
Did they believe the Magdalene whose Lord said
'Go and tell the others you have seen Me'
Could they believe the message of the Cross. The tomb. The Resurrection
Only one poor heart was not deceived, alone in the certainty of this day
Did they believe the new men at Pentecost
Who seemed as though they had drunk too much wine
The Lord is true to all He said. He is Risen
And returned now to His Father and His Spirit is for all people to receive
No man can defeat the Lord our God who is all
Did they believe the simple seers at Fatima not long ago
Did they believe the chosen soul of Bernadette at Lourdes
Doubting because they could not also see
Does our Blessed Mother come so far - so often - for no reason
Many saints have suffered from the disbelief of others
For man limits God to his own thinking and fails to see God is all
God's timing is perfect
Who sees all ways. Who sees all hearts. And does all things
So the humble may believe

Lean on God

Lean not on man but lean on God alone
He loves you and wants you as His own
There is a place awaiting and prepared
By going through the fire you will be spared

Lean on God. Give Him all your time
And in the blackest hour His light will shine
Like life anew delivered from the womb
Like Lazarus stepping from the tomb

The heart is like a flower is to rain
That closes on itself when feeling pain
Like shutters cutting out the air we breathe
That stunts the growth of life we could conceive

In Baptism the seed is planted deep
When ripen such a harvest you will reap
But like the meadow first must know the fire
In suffering God grants our hearts desire

God who loves His children equally
Measures out His love accordingly
The tallest tree drinks deeper just to live
More abundant in its fruit. More to give

There is no rest once this seeking has been sought
O how jealously He guards our every thought!
Lean not on man but lean on God alone
He loves you and wants you as His own

Whoever walks in darkness, and has no light shining for him,
let him trust in the name of Yahweh,
let him lean on his God. Is.50:10

Here I Am Lord

Here I am Lord, only me
Standing all alone
Your fields are where I rest
Heaven as my home

How simple is Your teaching
To stand upon Your word
Claiming all You say
Confessing You as Lord

Our footsteps intermingle
Where two is only one
Trust be the only step
In all You take me from

Here I am Lord, only me
Mindful of Your word
Standing in Your gift of Peace
Serving Christ my Lord

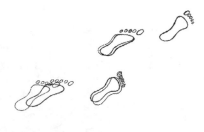

'I Yahweh, have called you to serve the cause of right;
I have taken you by the hand
and formed you.' Is.42:6

Our Father

Our Father who art in Heaven
Yet whose Spirit is in my soul
To Whom all things are possible
Within this earthly fold

Our Father who in Spirit
Can move Your unseen Hand
Break down the barriers of men
The meekest to the grand

Your power is unlimited
Your force that guides the wind
The same that holds the universe
And makes the seas mans' friend

You govern all the seasons
Whose timely harvests bring
Sufficient for all people
Through summer to the spring

Our Father who in Heaven
Can see this earth below
Lend all Your power to open
The minds of all to 'know'

Our Father who art in Heaven
Who gives each day we live
As You forgive our trespasses
So teach us to forgive

Deliver us from evil
Reveal Our Lady's way
Because You are our Father
And answer as we pray

Never Let Me Forget, Lord

Never let me forget Lord
The death You died for me
Let me remember always
The Cross on Calvary

The hill, the crowds, Your suffering
Your pain, Your loss of blood
Let me always come before You
And remember as I should

Your scourged flesh. Your crown of thorns
Such cruelty You met
The hands and feet that You hung by
Never, O Lord, let me forget

The mystery, the reason, for coming to this earth
To redeem us and to conquer sin, offering man new birth

O God who tells the rains to come, the sun to rise and fall
Look with pity on this world, have mercy on us all

How good You are to give this life. Who could deserve Your Son
He came so freely to poor man, not refusing anyone

Constantly remind me
Of this new path He gave
The Eternal Door that conquered death
How insignificant the grave!

Never let me forget Lord
This grace that I have known
When You, God's only Son
Died as if for me alone

Such cruelty You met

On Him lies the punishment that brings us peace,
and through His wounds we are healed. Is.53:5

The Living God

O Father of mankind who always was
Who has spoken to His people through the age
Who wrote my book of life and knows its end
Let me lead my life as written on each page

This book is held within Your Loving Hands
Each day revealing how my life should be
Open and awaiting in that place
Where You shower down Your word so constantly

When God speaks, a Voice from the Heavens,
Banished and removed is any doubt
If we obey, keeping faith with His word
Almighty God will bring all things about

How good You are to bring us to Your mountain
Like Abraham and Moses knew Your Voice
The same that commanded Noah to build the ark
And led the Blessed Virgin to rejoice

You prepare us for a task so tenderly
Leading and guiding as we seek
How patiently You await the response
From each child You make whose task is all unique

O Father of mankind who always was
Who has spoken to His people through the age
Who wrote my book of life and knows its end
Let me lead my life as written on each page

Only faith can guarantee the blessings that we hope for,
or prove the existence of the realities that at present remain unseen.
It was for faith that our ancestors were commended. Heb.11:1-2

Abba, Father

A single child of God caught beneath the Father's gaze
Tempered by His love having learnt His ways

A simple child of God who wears her Master's cloak
No burden weighing down. All sweetness in His yoke

A peaceful child of God
Sheltered by her Lord
In giving all of self
How rich is the reward

A child who learnt to soar
In the shadow of His wings
Rejoicing with praise
Of all the future brings

Who trusted in her Father's Hand
Whose only hope was He
Who walked upon the waters
And calmed the mighty sea

Who rescued her and carried her
Safely into harbour
To find eternal rest
And call Him 'Abba Father'

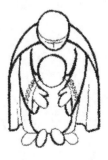

'Do not be afraid, for I have redeemed you;
I have called you by your name, you are mine.' Is.43:1

The Holy Spirit's Dwelling Place

Let there be no place in me
where You do not dwell
And healing waters ever flow
to say all is well
Let there be no place in me
where You do not shine
As Your adopted child
and Holy Spirit's shrine

Let me be like the glorious lilies
in Your field
That to Your power and grace
gladly yield
O Abba, Father, You know us
through and through
We make no move, no thought, no sigh
but through You

Let there be no place in me
where You would not meet
A gladdened will bended
to Your mercy seat
Let there be no place in me
where You do not reign
Surrendered to the Blood, the Cross,
the Lamb slain

Let there be nothing in me Lord
that You would spurn
That does not daily from Your Cross
a lesson learn
Let there be no place, O Holy Spirit,
found in me
That is not built as a Temple
fit for Thee

Having sought Your precepts I shall walk in all freedom.
Your commandments fill me with delight, I love them deeply.
Ps 119:45; 47

If Ever You Would Leave Me Lord

If ever You would leave me Lord, how could I bear the pain
Of travelling alone and living all in vain

If ever You would leave me Lord, to vanish from my side
Wherever would I seek comforting and Guide

If ever You abandoned me, leaving me alone
A void would fill my life and nowhere be my home

If ever You deserted me, my heart would lose its aim
And wither like a flower thirsting for the rain

A soul so full of love can tell of life reborn in You
While singing out Your praises of promises made true

With You in me and me in You journeying is sweet
And days are gladly offered as garlands at Your feet

Days of joy and faith and hope, of silence and of prayer
The stillness of Your Presence with Peace that fills the air

If ever You would leave me Lord, life would seem like death
Living as a corpse tormented by each breath

No never would You leave me Lord, who died for love of me
The Master of my soul, won so tenderly

Never will You leave me Lord. Nor would I part from Thee
Christ as my Beloved, God for Company

Jesus said, 'Know that I am with you always,
yes, to the end of time.' Mt.28:20

New Wine

Make us the work of Your hands Lord
Make us fruit of the vine
Crushing out impurities to become everlasting wine

Gods' children born from above
May carry no blemish within
Growing in grace and holiness, giving all things to Him

Like branches must be pruned
Thrown to everlasting fire
Here belongs our hidden will, our thoughts, our pride, desire

May the goodness found in Your mercy
Make us whole, and pure, complete
Transformed into glorious wine, mature, everlastingly sweet

Let Me Live

Let me live, and work for You, my God
Even though it seems against the tide
Let me strive for what is right, bringing others into Light
With You, Lord, walking ever at my side

Let me live for You and glorify Your name
With strength You give to combat every foe
For when God is on our side, His Love cannot be denied
Your Spirit, Lord, remains in me wherever I go

O Let me live this life You offer me
Rejoicing in Your will each rising day
This life You freely give, is life I gladly live
For You, Lord, answered me and came to stay

Steps of Faith

Searching ….. Finding

Finding ….. Knowing

Knowing ….. Hearing

Hearing ….. Doing

Doing ….. Witnessing

Witnessing ….. Gathering

Gathering ….. Community

Community ….. God's Kingdom come

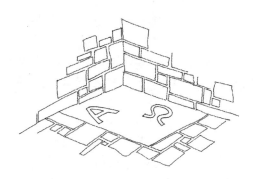

Jesus said, 'Look, the kingdom of God is among you.'
Lk.17:21

The Living Church

God is building a House upon Christ
The Foundation is solid built on rock
With the Word of the Shepherd who is Lord
To lead and be Protector of His flock

A Church where one can freely turn to pray
In unity with a fellow man
Centred upon Jesus as the Head
As at Pentecost where it all began

To proclaim the Good News to the poor
To turn the world about to love His name
Bringing justice, integrity and peace
And live as if today Christ comes again

Knowing Christ has died and Christ is Risen
Now crucified with Him being one
Asking anything of Him we may need
To the glory of the Father through His Son

To know the splendour of the Risen Lord
Through the darkness of the tomb to Heaven's gate
To listen to God's Spirit in our heart
As we gather in His name. And wait

To be in accordance with His holy will
Obedient to God before all man
Allowing God to prove to us His might
In our weakness as He unfolds His plan

*You are part of a building that has the apostles
and prophets for its foundations, and Christ Jesus Himself
for its main cornerstone. Eph.2:20*

Prayer of the Pilgrim Church

You go your way and I'll go mine
If they come together then let us combine
Our gifts and our talents, our labour and skill
Working while seeking God's holy will

You travel your way and I'll travel mine
Should they come together then let us combine
Our faith and our hope, all dreams that were tossed
In sorrow and joy not counting the cost

If His way is yours and His way is mine
They but come together to inter-twine
The path that our Saviour has called us upon
Daring in answer to follow God's Son

This road can be strewn with brambles and thorns
Dark waters that threaten and uncaring storms
But who comes towards us, upheld on the lake
Jesus! Who suffered and rose for our sake

This road can be also strewn with wild flowers
Their fragrance so rare, forgetful of hours
Where petals are gathered whenever we meet
For a garland of Love to place at His feet

A heart that has heard would abandon all
When God's voice has spoken in response to His call
There is but one way to walk, one direction to go
To tread in His footsteps left here below

So if your hands and my hands can toil side by side
With the Spirit to urge and our Mother to guide
Then we walk together the Pilgrim Way
That leads to our Father, our strength and our stay

'Remain in My Love'

Remain in My Love. Remain in My Love
That place you have come to know so well
My Body is a resting place where you must always stay
Your soul a holy Temple where I dwell

Remain in My Love. Remain in My Love
Remain with waters flowing freely from My side
Healing and restoring you, blessing you with power
That place in Me where nothing is denied

Remain in Me. Remain in Me
You are a constant witness to My Son
Whose death is never wasted in obedience to Me
Contrary to the belief of anyone

By fullness of My Word is man redeemed
My Gospel must be taken as a whole
Not by one of choice but by My every Word
I purify and sanctify the soul

Remain in Me. Remain in Me
Listen to the Voice you know the best
Is this a price too high to pay your Jesus crucified
And still the wine is flowing from My breast

My Living Waters never will run dry
Man can come to Me and have his fill
This everlasting Life I give, like flowing of the wine
Finds movement in the heart keeping still

Remain in Me. Remain in Me

*Jesus said, 'Remain in My love. If you keep My commandments
you will remain in My love,
just as I have kept My Father's commandments
and remain in His love.' Jn.15:9-10*

How Precious You Are

How precious you are to God your Father
For love of you He sent His only Son
He knows of each worry and confusion
And already sees the weary battle done
How precious you are to God your Father
Ponder on each loving word He said
He longs to comfort you in your distress
And waits to place a crown upon your head

How tenderly He watched you run this race
He guided you and blest you from the start
Each obstacle He moves and paves the way
To the prize that burns with His Sacred Heart
How precious you are to God your Father
He gave His Beloved Son to make you win
The death He died for you on Calvary
Claims victory and power over sin

How precious we are to God our Father
We glorify His name by being still
As Mary knew her place throughout her life
In peace accomplishing His will
How precious is Jesus to His Father
How we adore and praise His holy name
In confessing Him as Lord and Saviour
Of these simple souls to which His Spirit came

Blessed is anyone who perseveres when trials come.
Such a person is of proven worth and will win the prize of life,
the crown that the Lord has promised to those who love Him. Jm.1:12

The Gifts

The power that filled the Upper Room
can fill our mind
To seek and to receive His Son
is God's design

The Risen Lord gave His Peace to the Apostles
Then at Pentecost they gathered to await
The Dove that came as tongues of fire
The Force that no evil can penetrate

The Spirit of Truth descends. The Advocate
Revealing all things Jesus prophesied
Empowering to heal. To teach and pray
To know the mind of Christ. To touch His side

To be Fearful at the trumpet call of God
Hidden from His sight if we fail
He lends His holy Arm and mighty Hand
To draw and deliver through travail

We need Wisdom to read and know the Word
To interpret the way God speaks to us
How complicated is the thinking of mankind
Destroying simple faith and hope and trust

God sends Fortitude to be the inner strength
To enable us to witness for His sake
Obedient to God before all man
Protected from the enemies we make

We need to Understand our Father's way
His discipline. How strict are His commands
Because He is God and knows all things
There is purpose in all that He demands

He gives Knowledge of His Son when faith is proven
The very height of Heaven, width and length
He gives Counsel, empowering with His Light
When it seems we might be tried beyond our strength

The Humility of Christ our greatest Teacher
The Kingliest of all. Yet so meek
Though equal to His Father took His Cross
Showing us the Poverty we seek

The Spirit shows the Father loving Son
The Beloved in Whom He is well pleased
The Father's will the pleasure of the Son
Who by His very power was conceived

When the Spirit comes He takes us to Himself
In Holiness and Purity He dwells
The still and listening heart is opened wide
To God's secrets and the mysteries He tells

There appeared to them tongues as of fire;
these separated and came to rest on the head of each of them.
They were all filled with the Holy Spirit. Acts 2:3-4

O Gentle Flame of Love

O Gentle flame of love within my soul
Lead me ever on towards my destiny
May I move ever closer to that meeting
A time beyond today awaiting me

O Burning flame of love within my soul
Melting all my will till Yours is done
Enkindling in me Your very strength
Who led me to this day, lead kindly on

O Glowing flame of love that never darkens
May You shine while I diminish in this world
Send forth Your beam to guide beyond this path
Where Your plan so long prepared is unfurled

Lord, Lord, may You be recognised as He
Whose wondrous Law of Love is without limit
The Living God speaking to His people
To the praise and glory of the Holy Spirit

In this still time of prayer increase my trust
Every comfort or place of refuge is denied
Abandoning myself to You alone
With every part of my own will crucified

O Gentle shield of God who touches me
Who is my Rock, my Fortress and my Stay
Carry me into the bright tomorrow
O Lead me kindly on, I pray

You can say to Yahweh 'My refuge, my fortress,
my God in whom I trust!' Ps.91:2

'Neath Our Lady's Mantle

'Neath Our Lady's mantle
Is where I'll ever be
Remembering that God
Once rested on her knee

'Neath the Cross of Jesus
Is where I'll ever stay
Recalling how Mary
Stood there with Him that day

'Neath the Father's gaze
Who would not want to be
Following with Mary
Enrapt in mystery

God who in His mercy
In ways that could not seem
Gave to us as Mother
The ever-Virgin Queen

'Neath Mary's mantle
With tenderness so rare
Is where I'll stay with Jesus
In His mother's care

Jesus said 'Behold your mother.' Jn.19:27

Such Loss

Its black. Its bleak
I'm cold. And weak
And the heaviest weight I've ever known
is hanging
where my heart should be

Its true. Its real
this way I feel
And the saddest time I've ever known
lies ahead
That is all I see

For a time
you were mine
And the greatest joy I'd ever known
resounded
all inside of me

Now you are gone
I'm dead. I'm numb
Such ghastly emptiness before unknown
is here
where my child should be

Life goes on
my little one
Just silence and the stillest prayer I've ever prayed
that alone
can my grief afford

Through tears somehow
I see you now
How bitter-sweet to know that you, my love,
enjoy
the Presence of my Lord

The Cross

When you pick up your Cross and its heavy
Through loneliness or fear
Now is the time to remember
Jesus is specially near

Learning the Cross is a lesson
Christ Jesus taught the best
Staying one with the Father
Leads the soul to rest
We feel God all the nearer
In darkness or a threat
Training us to stray not from
The Kingdom we have met

In some God sees a diadem, a jewel oh so rare
From these He asks some sacrifice. Could other Love compare
He gives sweet consolation, true vision and pure sight
Knowledge of His only Son to make the Cross more light

Within the Cross is Christ with grace like morning dew
The power to rise to God with Life born anew
When the Cross is laden with extra-ordinary trial
How thankful is the soul to feel His Presence all the while

When life is all surrendered
He is ever close to care
And the Cross becomes a blessing
Just because He is there
For humble is His Majesty
This mighty King of Kings
He bends so low to tend us
And gives the soul new wings

Since there is no returning
From this journey once begun
With this mystical uniting
God marks His chosen one
The Cross is daily carried
With Love to never part
When He has caught and captured
The sanctuary of the heart

Detachment

I see you, loving you as ever
I see you from whichever way I stand
You're not with me, but very far away
Led by our Father's touch and mighty Hand

Here I am, loving you as always
I cared for you, watched you grow along the way
I see you, loving from a distance
With pride and joy no one can take away

For a while you belonged to me
For a while you were truly mine
Then came the wonder of the Holy Spirit
Inviting to share His quest Divine

God calls to a place where paths diverge
And love reveals itself in words unspoken
To bravely bear the parting of the ways
And follow in His steps with faith unbroken

I see you, loving you as ever
Our separate paths will unite again
But I watched you turn away and disappear
Praying God would fill the void and heal the pain

For God is with me as He is with you
He is loving me in this place where I am
Pleased when His beloved children answer 'Yes'
And enter into His mysterious plan

Whether you are at my side or far away
A plenteous supply of grace comes from Him
Who sees beyond the passages of time
And sends His holy love to flow within

Desire for Baptism

Rid me of my nature Lord so I may come to Thee
I want to live in Heaven with You
But I don't want to live with me!

Rid me of my nature Lord. Change me, make me new
Clothe me in a garment of white. Oh make me more like You

Wash away all sin and guilt. Cleanse me, make me whole
With Living Waters purify. Sanctify my soul

Holy Mother, pray for me. I know that this is true -
God's children can be free from sin - for He has shown us you

So take my fallen nature Lord. Shine Your Light in me
Let Your Holy Spirit teach all I am meant to be

Rid me of my selfishness. Let me leave behind
Ways that are displeasing. Ways to which I'm blind

Take from me all You reject. Don't leave me as I am
I want to be included in Your ever loving plan

Take my fallen nature Lord
Place in me Your own
So I am welcome with the Saints
To worship round Thy throne

Seek First the Kingdom of God

Seek first the Kingdom of God
Keep Him first on your list
Keep Him shining ahead like a light
Throughout every turn and twist

Seek first the Kingdom of God
Keep the Lord on His throne
Come let our Beloved Christ
Make your troubles His own

He longs to take your sorrow
And gather it to His breast
He longs to heal your hurt
And to your soul give rest

Pray to God always. But first
Offer Him praise day and night
Let the thought of His Kingdom
Be paramount in your sight

Seek first the Presence of God
Cast doubt and fear aside
Banish all thought of darkness
Mistrust, despair and pride

Give to Him glory and honour
Keep Him first in your mind
Never give up. Jesus promised
His Kingdom is there to find

Seek Him, call to Him, pester Him
Whatever the hour may be
If we knock He will open the door
That door to Eternity

The Present Moment

I don't want to wait till I'm old, Lord, to appreciate Your world
This fragile world You gave into our care
I don't want to wait till tomorrow
Till everything is too late
Today I want to make a difference everywhere

I don't want to wait till I'm old, Lord, to learn to give You thanks
I want to be aware of all that You have done
I don't want to wait until the end
To discover how You died
And hung there for me as if I were the only one

Lord, I don't want to wait till it's too late to do Your will each day
The will You made so long ago for me
I want to know You through all things
Each present moment Lord
And touch Your Life in everything I know and hear and see

I don't want to wait till I'm old, Lord, to appreciate my life
This life You have created from the start
When all the world was silent
Even then You thought of me
Wanting to place Your Spirit within my heart

You don't have to wait till I'm old, Lord, till my voice sings out in prayer
I gladly come to You to offer praise
All the present, future and the past
Is totalled in Your Word
Impressing You in me for all my days

You don't have to wait till I'm old, Lord, for me to turn to You
For each moment is spent in You somehow
To the glory of the Father
Through Jesus Christ who gave
The indwelling of His Spirit here and now

Can You Remember

Can you remember the feel
of the blade of grass beneath your feet
Can you remember running along
touching flowers smelling oh so sweet

Can you remember when something small
seemed oh so large, so big, so vast
When someone else knew the answer
to every question you ever asked

Can you remember being taken along
to Church or Chapel or prayer
Being told everything was simple
For God was here. And everywhere

Can you remember
seeing a sunrise over the land
Thinking how very beautiful is that made by God's own Hand

Can you remember wondering why people were sad and cried
Had everyone forgotten the message Jesus left as He died
Can you remember learning of war and wounds and pain
And thinking whatever would our Saviour say
if He came to earth again

Can you remember what happened
from the ways that were till today
How everything now seems scattered
and some have chosen another way
Can you remember saying
'This is the way I shall go
I feel happy and safe and secure
in the Faith I love and know'

Can you remember the day
when you stood before God alone
And made that decision to stay
answerable to His throne

Remember some things never change
like the feel of the sun on your face
The only real things of importance
are God's power, His Love, His grace

If you can remember the sun that shines
is the same that shone on Christ
It brings all things around to see
the positive side of life

Do you recollect a broken heart
and wished all pain would cease
And pray and yearn and hope and believe
that world would live in peace
Jesus said the only way
is through Him who died for us all
To see Him present in everything,
each day, each event we recall

Can you remember the joy so great
it took all hurting and tears - even the pain of grieving – away
That place of healing and peace and Love
is where we live for ever,
together,
united for always
One day. One day

I Wonder What It Feels Like

I wonder what it feels like to fly in the air unhindered, unfettered,
to dance and soar on the wing
I wonder what it feels like to have what you want, to go anywhere,
to be a princess or a king

I wonder what it feels like to stand on the moon and then through my eyes
look back at the distance to earth
Or to know what will happen from beginning to end
to each person to death from their birth

I wonder how it feels to be great or small, to be rich, or poor but still me
To be famous, unknown, sought after or shunned, imprisoned
to be then set free

I wonder how it feels to understand, to be fluent
with every language ever spoken
To know every heart and mind, every hair on each head
since the world began, since Creation herself was awoken

I wonder how it feels not to move or sing, to be deaf or blind or dumb
The crippled, the broken, the lost, the poor - to God
each is His shining one

I wonder how it feels to know one day soon life will come to an end
living on time that we only can borrow
To think in our heart this night is my last
to really know we won't be here tomorrow

I wonder what it's like not to believe in our loving God
Who forgives and restores as we ask
To take sin and shame and guilt and pride
for Him is a loving task

The reason He gave so long ago, to care, to be, to live, to die
this He showed, revealed, to all men
When He gave to the world His Beloved Son
Who heals, Who forgives, Who as Love came to love not condemn

I know what it's like to experience pain, loss, gladness and joy
also to experience living in God's grace
The more open the heart the more one can receive
the Look, that ravishing Look, from God's Face

On this earth we can have a foretaste of glory to come
of some portion of Love take part
To hold all He offers kept vacant for 'me'
we embrace all He says, daily entering His Heart

For in Him we have a great High Priest who for our sake became as we are
Without sin, with love, with truth He came, no false glory or pride
The Sacrifice made, a new Covenant given
by His wounds on the Cross, by tears that He shed
by the Blood that flowed from His side

For our great High Priest, God's only Son, has gone ahead to gather us all
everyone, near or far
He has undergone everything, emptied Himself and in tenderness says
'I love you and know who you are.'

*It is not as if we had a high priest who was incapable
of feeling our weaknesses with us, but we have one who has been tempted
in every way that we are, though He is without sin. Heb.4:15*

Do You Know How Deeply You Are Loved

Do you know how deeply you are loved

Imagine every little child cradled in one pair of arms
That amount of love flows down to you
Imagine every person's smile as if from one alone
Coming from but one Source, one eye, one view

God loves His children with a never-ending Love

More deeply than a lover, higher than a mountain climbed
Longer than any story ever told
Bluer than the bluest sky, wider than the widest sea
Richer than any treasures eyes could behold

O Think how deeply you are loved

God sent His Son into the world, tangible and true
Bridging all the bounds of time and space
Spanning all the centuries and galaxies and stars
To be more familiar to you than your own face

O See how deeply you are loved

God promised to be with us, every corner of the earth
Covering every spot from east to west
He is all above, beyond, around us, yet within
So fear and any doubt can know His rest

O See how deeply you are loved

O Child of Mine

O Child of mine within my womb how peaceful you lie there
While so deeply cherished rest without a care

The life I give will help you grow, the life I give will nourish
The warmth and tenderness you feel will bless you as you flourish

Unknowing child with un-thought thoughts, innocent and pure
Gather all the strength you can for tests you must endure

Someday soon my time will come of making you your own
When you will be no part of me and travel the unknown

I love you while I still have time to feel you deep within
My caress is just as sure as the awaited quickening

Too soon will separation come. Too soon the time to part
Though you are gone a sign will be remaining in my heart

For what seems one will then be two. This womb that was your home
These loving arms that sheltered you can't hold you when you're grown

O child of God, within my womb
slumber while you can
So quick your steps will turn away
the child becoming man

For from these empty arms you knew will come the space to shine
And I will ever thank the Lord that He has made you mine

Slumber while you can

The Eyes of a Child

Did you ever look into the eyes of a child, What did you see there
Joy and love and hope and trust revealing endless care
Have you ever looked into the eyes of a child to wonder what could have been
The reason for their starkness. What misery have they seen

Eyes reflect the soul. They mirror that within
Images created by that done to her or him

The eyes of a child see terror in war and death each day
All another child owns taken cruelly away

Some live in isolation, locked in hate or fear
While others live in luxury, crying but a selfish tear

Some children live in hospitals, wards they never leave
Others know radiation in every breath they breathe

For some home is an orphanage. From some, Love hid and kept
Some caused to suffer deliberately. O See why Jesus wept

Some children never learn of their Eternal inheritance
Though securely educated in every other sense

Being denied the knowledge of this opportunity
Whatever powers enchain them to be inwardly set free

Some children live in squalor or where bombings never cease
Some live and die not having heard the silent sound of peace

Innocence is stolen, burdens placed upon
Our little ones who lives are aged before they hardly have begun

That one true place of sanctuary, once haven of the womb
Now seeks to end a life violated oh so soon

Did you ever look into the eyes of a child. What did you see there
Joy and hope and love and trust revealing endless care
Have you ever looked into the eyes of a child to wonder what could have been
The reason for their starkness. What misery have they seen

We owe each child a future as bright as the brightest star
Each child that lives, those yet unborn, regardless of who or where they are

Whenever we look into the eyes of a child we should only ever see
A look that beams and says 'I love, for someone has loved me.'

I Know Him

I knew Him when I was a child
Read of Him. Spoke of Him. Prayed to Him

I heard Him call when I was alone
He freed me. He saved me. He healed me

I followed Him gladly each day I lived
To praise Him. Serve Him. Adore Him

He is the Way, the Truth, the Life
He is Jesus. Risen. I met Him

I follow Him still each day on earth
He is living. He is with me. I know Him

Jesus Lives

Look around and you will see
Jesus lives in you and me

Look within and you will find
Jesus in your heart and mind

Our Blessed Lord who came to give
His own life that we may live

Always, ever, at His side
Through the Church He calls His bride

Sing to Him, His praises tell
And with Him in glory dwell

He is ever deep within
Keeping pure and free from sin

In His home He gladly stays
Pouring forth His healing rays

Jesus brings His life to me
Promising eternity

Love that comes, Love that is
He is mine and I am His

Jesus lives   *Jesus*   Jesus lives

I Have Met You

I have met You. I have met You. I know that You are there
I love you, I love you. I know You hear my prayer

I have met You, Lord. I met You. I know that You are here
You cast away all darkness and freed my soul from fear

I know You. I sense You, my Saviour, my King
Real Presence, true God of Whom I'll ever sing

I have met You, I have met You on this altar here adored
I shall meet You once again my Ever-Living Lord

I have met You, I have touched You, I have held Your life in mine
I have met You, and enraptured answered Love Divine

I came to You. You come to me in the stillness of my heart
Wedded to that place in me never to depart

I have listened. You have spoken. Your Voice in me was heard
I bowed down and adored You, my Lord, Incarnate Word

I have met You, O My Jesus. Here Your glory reigns
Your Body feeds my soul. Your Blood runs through my veins

I have met You, and I meet You because You live in me
Father, Son and Spirit, most Blessed Trinity

Freedom

Freedom is sweet liberty
I give to God to use
He never imposes His will on mine
I can accept
Or can refuse

God never invades that space in me
He gave me as my own
But how pleased is He, how blessed am I
How royal in me
His throne

When I discover He knows best
And let His will be done
I give to God all I am to be
More like
His Beloved Son

Freely given, freely received
In glad surrender till
My God who made both Heaven and earth
Creates
A perfect will

For once He came, by night a fire
A pillar of cloud by day
In the form of a Dove God now descends
And Heaven once more
Has its sway

Follow Christ

Follow Christ, to His path be true
He shed His blood and made all things new

His glory He shines. His Spirit He sends
He shares His own Life which never ends

This secret is born in hearts that are pure
He gives Divine Guidance and grace to endure

There is a path that bids all 'Come'
Where footprints sink in to those of the Son

With Faith for a staff and Joy for a crown
His Holy Presence a radiant gown

The Bride has 'Come'. The Groom is here
O Blessed meeting. To Christ draw near

A welcome awaits. None turned away
Who truly tread the Saviour's way

Jesus said, 'Come follow Me.'

Upon Good Friday

Upon Good Friday I was bereft
Upon Good Friday how I wept

They took my Saviour. They took my King
They took my Jesus, my everything

With wounds inflicted around His head
They left Him hanging, wanting Him dead

Upon Good Friday they took my Lord
Opened His heart with piercing sword
As Blood and water gushed from His side
Brazen man 'The Christ' denied

Salvation lost. God's promise undone
If they can kill the Anointed One
His only Son. No more to send
Nothing can save us. This must be the end

All breath is gone now. Hopes disappear
The Word is crushed by those who jeer
Who recognised Him hanging there
Cold as the grave. Death in the air

I saw my Jesus. Veiled with Blood
I recognised Him from where I stood
Upon Good Friday torment, loss
Nothing left. O cruel Cross

He Is Risen From the Grave

He is Risen from the grave
Our God who came to save
Triumphant over death is He
Though this life is fleeting
How blest it is by meeting
Jesus, Lord, who reigns eternally

While splend'rous is His throne
He came to make His own
The people who once walked without light
His radiance He shed
On the living and the dead
Delivering our souls in tender fight

By ourselves the battle is lost
He came to pay the cost
We can but receive from all He gives
And step into His power
O What amazing hour
When Jesus rose and showed us that He lives

Jesus offers us this Gift
His sword is sure and swift
He longs for us. He died to set us free
He will mercifully give
His grace that we might live
And shines His light for everyone to see

Thank the Father for the Son
Whose victory was won
As Jesus surrendered to His will
And by His holy Flame
We rely upon His name
And Blood spilt by the Lamb upon that Hill

He Bore the Weight

He bore the Cross. He bore the weight
To conquer death and fear and hate
He bore our lives upon the Tree
So we live today with souls set free

He bore the shame. He bore the weight
So we may know a sinless state
A child of God lives free from sin
Drinking grace supplied by Him

The gift to choose to do God's will
He purchased as He climbed the hill
He shows us how to give our all
How to obey God's certain call

Long ago He carried me
Borne was I on Calvary
He learnt as Son through suffering
Took us beneath God's Sacred Wing

Claiming us as He was killed
Saving us by Blood He spilled
This new Life before unknown
Wrought by Christ, by Christ alone
He paid the price entering then
A New Covenant with hearts of men
So I may live unburdened, free
He bore the Cross, loving me

Made into sin, the 'Undefiled'
That I become my Father's child
Regaining all God's blessedness
To live in praise and thankfulness

This happened then so far away
And yet is Present here today

Jesus! Master!

Jesus! Master! God on high
Lord of Heaven, earth, sea and sky

Universal Lord and King
We hail Your name and praises sing

Precious One who once was slain
Spread Your Light from where You reign

O Majesty. Victorious
Teach this world You died for us

When on the clouds for all to see
Jesus! Master! Come for me

Purest Lamb. Love outpoured
Holy Head. Scorned. Adored

Emptied. Buried. Powerless
Beauty. Grace. God no less

Bleeding Heart and gaping Side
Made the Church Your holy bride

O Pierced One. O Wounded Flame
Prepare that Day You come again

O Pelican, whose Love for me
Holds fast within sweet mystery!

The pelican, having a red tip at the end of its beak, became a symbol of self-sacrifice in medieval Europe, for by this red tip the pelican drew blood from its own breast as nourishment for its young.

In ecclesiastical symbolism, the pelican vulning (wounding) itself represents the Church feeding Her children with Her life. Its highest symbolic significance is reached when used as an emblem of Christ, whose Blood was poured out for mankind, and who daily gives Himself as the nourishment for our souls in the Blessed Sacrament.

Such expression can be found in the hymn 'Adore te Devote' – 'O Godhead Hid' (by St Thomas Aquinas) referring to Jesus as 'Loving Pelican' with blood so powerful one drop is enough for an entire world's ransoming.

Faith, Hope and Charity

Faith is that
which believes and moves mountains
coaxing, persuading to keep *Hope* alive

That beautiful Gift
God gives to His servant
one without which I would not want to survive

Hope is that
which gives purpose and meaning
to days which would be otherwise
bleak and grey

Faith whispers to *Hope*
'Let us not diminish
but grow stronger, deeper and more fervent each day'

Faith and *Hope*
can together transform us
bring vision, power and strength from above

Given light and reason
to then complete
God fills to the brim with His mystical *Love*

Jesus Wept

Jesus wept as He stood and prayed over Jerusalem
Longing to gather close to Him the souls of men

Jesus wept upon the death of His friend Lazarus
With the same immensity of love He bears for us

Jesus wept. Only by returning to the Father's side
Only by His passion could the Spirit present the bride

Jesus longed to share the Passover, to take the path He trod
Accomplishing His mission with confidence in God

Jesus wept over all God's children, including you and me
By His holy wounds we are healed. So wondrously!

Jesus wept with love for man by which His heart was gripped
His Sacred Body spat upon, torn and mocked and whipped

Jesus died. Though God, like any man He feared
Sweating drops of blood as His crucifixion neared

God wept. The consequence of sin made Jesus weep
He undertook the Cross to awaken man from sleep

God's Mother wept, Mary, 'The Immaculate Conception'
Whose body, blood, faith, for us had fed 'The Resurrection'

How deep the mystery of God made man on earth
The mystery of Jesus coming in human birth

Jesus won! Glory be to Him! Might and Majesty!
Drawing us unto the Father through Calvary

Jesus rose! By His body on the Cross we are redeemed
Jesus knew He was the Son of God
And nothing was as it had seemed!

He Took My Place

He took my place on Calvary
Imagine doing this for me!

He took my place! What man is this
A man betrayed by Judas' kiss

He took my place! That cruel day
Murdered in an awful way

Mary mourned. Some shed a tear
Wicked men stood round to jeer

He took my place! What friend is He
A friend prepared to die for me

No pleasant death do nails afford
No comfort has my bleeding Lord

What Love He shows this heart of mine
Love so strong. Love divine

He took my place that I may live
With Love to keep and Love to give

To keep me pure and free from sin
So when I die I go to Him

He opened wide the door of death
Eternal life in His last breath

He took my place! What God is He
God, who died this death for me.

Did You See Him There

Did you see Him there
Or would you have been the one to run away and hide

Did you see Him there
Or would you have been the one to thrust the sword
into His side

Did you see His mother
Was your heart not moved with pity as she saw Him
hanging there

Did you see
Could you not sense the torment, the agony of mind
and despair

Did you see His blood
It flowed freely from His hands, down the Cross to His feet
Did you look into His eyes
Or was there something in them you would choose to avoid
and not meet

Did you not ask for pardon
Like one of the two thieves who were hanging there, either side
God loves us
His mercy is for all and breaks through every barrier. But pride

Were you frightened
The earth quaked, the rocks were split, the dead rose from their graves
Those around with the centurion realised they looked upon
the Son of God who saves

I think if I were there
I would ask Him, if He would, to take me with Him into Paradise
I would want to tend His wounds
to make certain He would never again become for us a Sacrifice

But did you see Him
Did you glance then carry on and wander off without a care
Or did you realise it was Jesus, our Lord, the Saviour of the world
hanging there

Blessed Trinity

O Father, Abba. Creator of all on earth we know
Omnipresent. Yet living in Your children here below

O Lord Jesus. Lover making all souls new
Not one thing has its being except is found in You

O Holy Spirit. Teacher of all from Heaven above
Bringing down burning Flame lighting up pure Love

Blessed Trinity. Giver of grace and life and light
Source of every blessing. Fount of all delight

Praise to You, O Heavenly Father. Praise to You, Beloved Son
Praise to You, dear Paraclete. All praises, Three-In-One

Help Me Lord!

Help me Lord!
Inspire me
Show me life anew
That I may praise and ever be
Closer
My Lord, to You

Help me Lord!
Look on me
Filling me anew
That I may shine and ever grow
Closer
My Lord, to You

Hear me Lord!
Bend my will
Give me Love anew
That I may serve and ever live
Closer
My Lord, to You

Take me Lord
Into Your Heart
Draw me next to You
That I may rise and ever want
My Lord,
to follow You

Lord Send Your Spirit

Lord send Your Spirit! Send Your fire!
Grant to man his heart's desire

Send Your Spirit! End this night
Breathe on us. Bring us alight

Conquer sin and evil's ways
Lord now set this world ablaze!

Send Your Spirit. Mighty sword!
Heal this land, O Living Lord

Send Your Spirit. Lead us through
Cause all man to turn to You

O Holy fire! Burning flame!
Melt all hearts. Call each by name

Sift us Lord. Your power increase
Till all hearts ask Your Peace

Fill us Spirit to the brim
Let Your power enter in

On us all, Lord, take Your hold
Let the future way unfold

Lord send Your Spirit. Holy Dove
Melt us in Your perfect Love

Lord send Your Spirit. Send Your grace
Let us seek You Face to face

There is a Place

There is a place where He lives
It is never very far
and it neither moves
nor disappears
with the night
It is here that He lives
buried deep within my heart
It never dims
but is for me
a constant light

There is a place where He lives
He knows that He is welcome
for He neither moves
nor disappears
with the day
It is here that He lives
buried deep within my heart
For I listen
to His Voice
as I pray

There is a place where He lives
which He has made His home
for He neither moves
nor disappears from within
It is here that my God
is eternally at home
In that place
which He knows
belongs to Him

The Cup We Share

The Cup we share is a new Covenant in His Blood
The Lamb slain
The Old is passed away. The New ever to remain

The Cup we take is a new Covenant in His Love
Love to bear
The new Command of Love demonstrated by His care

The Cup we taste is a new Covenant in His Life
For everyone
Complete and everlasting. It can never be undone

The Cup He gave is for washing in His Blood
Which frees us
Healing, keeping safely in the arms of Jesus

The Cup He offered is the final and eternal Covenant
For man
Prepared by God for all ages. Before time itself began

The Cup He took and raised within His Sacred hands
Was for me
That I might live and have some share in His Divinity

The Cup He drank at Supper, sensing betrayal
Death, loss
Was filled with Precious Blood that trickled down the Cross

The Cup He shed for mans' atonement
In everlasting memory
Sacred Lamb. Sacred wounds. The Cup poured out for me

The Cross Stands Over All the Earth

The Cross stands over all the earth
    For all to see
    It is there to raise us up
    Into Eternity

The Cross stands over everything
    Covering the earth
    We live in its power
    To death from our birth

The Cross stands high above
    We live in its shade
    Transforming us for God
    In whose image we are made

The Cross stands lifted high
    While earth below
    Radiates God's Love
    We live in its glow

The Cross is height supreme
    Yet depth of shame
    Being the instrument on which
    The Christ was slain

The Cross is before me
    O wondrous sight!
    Bridging earth to Heaven
    Shedding glorious light!

Now God's Will Is Done

There is Peace
Now God's will is done
And we can know His Presence
With each rising of the sun

There is Peace
Now God's Son has died
And we can know our Master
Dead and glorified

There is Peace
Now God's Son is Risen
And He can fill all emptiness
Through saving graces given

We have His Peace
God in us lives on
Mankind received His Peace
God sent His only Son

Jesus left Peace
That is why He came
To do the Father's will
And let His Peace reign

Let there be Peace
Jesus paid the price
By the mercy in Your wounds
Breathe on us, Peace of Christ

Jesus Walked on the Water

Jesus walked on the water at Galilee
What miracle of faith to believe
By reaching out to Him He reaches us
And walk with Him on waters to receive

Jesus fed the multitudes at Galilee
Acknowledging their need to be fed
He was able to satisfy their hunger
From just two fishes and five loaves of bread

The Risen Jesus appeared at Galilee
Preparing food for friends gathering there
They would Baptise through the Father, Son and Spirit
Not just in Galilee but everywhere

Jesus calmed the waters at Galilee
Jesus fed the crowds with more than bread
Jesus said He was the Son of God
And gave us proof by rising from the dead

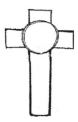

Jesus bids us walk with Him like Galilee
Sharing in a way no other could
Jesus left with us His very Self
Giving us His Body and His Blood

Our King Who Serves

Our Blessed Lord came to serve
Giving Love none could deserve
Our Blessed Lord came to save
Giving Life beyond the grave

Our Saviour showed humility
Not recognised. Such few could see
Our Saviour came to bless and heal
Giving joy none could steal
Bringing peace, the Spirit's sign
Being His. He being mine

Our Saviour came to set us free
To cure mankind's iniquity
Jesus came to be our Light
To vanquish darkness of the night
Our Lord is God yet did not swerve
From the Cross. He came to serve

He was King. The Word made flesh
With Living Waters to refresh
A King behaves differently
Who washes feet on bended knee
His Royal garment is not seen
Yet needs no sun from which to glean

This Son from Heaven gives pure rest
In souls where He alone is Guest
His humble state was Divine
Changing water into wine

With power to wash all sin away
And grace to live in Him each day
For as Scripture has unfurled
Our Saviour's Blood saved the world

This my King, my chosen Way
I'll follow Him and not delay
Our Blessed Lord did not swerve
He died for those He came to serve

Who Could Give Such Love

Who could give such Love but He
Who lives and reigns eternally

He who is the richest Source
And let all history run its course

Who but God could supply
Such amount when all is dry
There is no charge for such He gives
Through Jesus crucified who lives

The price was paid so long ago
When man was dead and did not know
Our Dear Lord would bring true Life
And rescue man from all his strife

His Peace He gave so all may be
One with Love hung on a tree
And redeemed from all his sin
Be ever free to turn to Him

All this Love so freely given
Lives in man when forgiven
So he may then in return
Serve Our Lord and from Him learn

Such Encounter! Sweet it is
Loving Christ and being His
On this earth Himself makes known
So that His Gospel Word be sown

And we receive the Love of He
Who lives and reigns eternally

Who Are We

Who are we to take the Cup He offers
Who are we to satisfy our thirst
Who are we that we can approach Him
It is so. Because God loved us first

Who am I to take the Cup He offers
It is He who makes me wonder why
He loves me and leads to me still waters
It is so. He feeds my soul when dry

Who are you to take the Cup He offers
Who is man that God keeps him in mind
Who but God could love us in His Son
It is so. Yet many hearts are blind

How can it be that we take and drink of Him
How can it be God raised us from the Fall
It is He whose Love is all embracing
It is so. God's mercy is for all

Who is He that He has come from Heaven
In mystery too great to comprehend
The Christ. The Very Son in flesh
True God. The Beginning and the End

Who are we to hear the sound of triumph
Who are we to have God's only Son
Who are we to share all He accomplished
It is so. His Victory is won!

Who is He who stands and is welcoming
Who is He who waits with open Heart
It is God, who made us for a purpose
It is so. Each has to play some part

Who are you to drink the Cup He offers
Who are you and who are they and who am I
God loves us wanting us for Jesus
It is so because God let Him die

Who are we to cry 'Holy Holy
Holy Lord, God of power and might'
We are Yours, O holy Lamb of God
Baptised! Beloved in Your sight

We are His, created in His image
Called in joy to celebrate with zeal
His disciples gathered around His table
It is so. We share His holy meal

So we come to Him when we are hungry
And come again in trust for Him to feed
It is He who gives to us Himself
It is so. Because He knows our every need

We come to Him to take the Cup He offers
With drink that satisfies our thirst
Who are we that we can approach Him
It is so. Because God loved us first

O Road to Emmaus

O Road to Emmaus! O path to my heart
Where Jesus beckoned to make this start

O Breaking of Bread! Giving life to my soul
Making me precious, renewed and whole

O Road to Calvary! Bitter sweet
Where life and death together meet

O Road to Emmaus! Where You have trod
I journey onwards facing my God

Starting with Moses and going all through the prophets,
He explained to them the passages throughout the Scriptures
that were about Himself. Lk.24:27

What Good Ever Came From Nazareth

What good ever came from Nazareth
That undeserving place
Where disbelief was written on each familiar face

What good could come from Nazareth so settled in its ways
Who could transform its people into witnessing with praise

Who could change their attitude in this village safe and sure
Where they failed to see the Lord for the simple cloak He wore
In that place which was His home, a carpenter's young Son
A place without renown where Salvation was begun

Jesus came from Nazareth seeking wealth nor fame
But to free us and redeem us by the power of His name
To bring us to the Kingdom such wonders there occurred
And brought about by Him, the Father's Living Word

And when He spoke in Nazareth His words met deafened ears
They refused to see their need. Refused to know their fears
So little was their faith in Him. So little could they see
How moved this man of God while roaming Galilee
Who cured the sick and evil, rebuking the oppressed
But He could work no miracle in those who 'knew' Him best

Our Saviour dwelt in Nazareth. He whom they refused
Was given over to Pilate like a criminal accused
Jesus came from Nazareth this man of 'no deceit'
Who wore our crown of thorns and had nails put in His feet

This man who dwelt in Nazareth, true hearts would not deny
Lives on today among us with Life that cannot die
Who came with faith to fill the earth revealing the unseen
Such goodness bears the Name - Jesus - the Nazarene!

Jesus and The Father

To know how Jesus loved the Father
is to have some small idea of how He wanted us to live
He showed us how to be at Peace with God and man. And to forgive

To see how Jesus loved the Father
is to have some small idea of how He wanted us to be
He lived His life in obedience. He is with us. And still today sets prisoners free

To hear how Jesus loved the Father
is to have some idea of how to become co-heirs with Him
Our Risen and inspiring joy! God, yet man, calls 'Come. Enter in'

To learn how Jesus loved the Father
is to have some idea of why He calls us by our name
The personal and abiding touch from Jesus, whose Victory we claim

To feel how Jesus loved the Father
is to burn with one desire and share the sufferings He bore
And ease His Love into another's soul whom He already has died for

To grasp how Jesus loved the Father
is to kneel at Calvary where the Lord heard ridicule and laugh
And follow His footsteps to Heaven where He intercedes on our behalf

To show how Jesus loved the Father
bears some reflection of how He gives sufficient grace
In a fallen world our Saviour reigns and God, to us, sheds glory from His Face

To love as Jesus loved the Father
is through the power of His Spirit, giving glory to the Trinity alone
Where His saints and choirs of angels, and His Virgin Mother
assist us to our Heavenly home. Amen

Addressing His Father, Righteous One, Jesus said,

I have made Your name known to them and will continue to make it known
so that the love with which You loved Me may be in them
and so that I may be in them.' Jn.17:26

It's Not Supposed to Be Like This

It's not supposed to be like this
Lord, where did I go wrong
For every step feels heavy
And every road seems long

It's not supposed to be this way. It's rather dread and drear
What happened Lord to happiness. Where did it disappear

Lord, how is it supposed to be. How does the darkness start
I fear that I might suffer an eclipsing of the heart

The Cross, Lord, is affecting me. It's causing me some pain
I feel like I have fallen and must learn to walk again

I thought I knew the answers, but now I'm at a loss
I feel the awful weight of carrying my cross

Where is that place I'm certain of abundant Love for me
O send Your Holy Spirit. Let Him my comfort be

O Lord, He brings such glorious Light
Now I can see Him shine
Ah! It's supposed to be
Your will, Lord. Not mine!

Jesus said, 'Yes, My yoke is easy
and My burden is light.' Mt.11:30

Where There is Love

Where there is Love God is living
Hidden in the joy of simple giving

Where there is Love God is around
In the gentlest breeze and softest sound

God is near when tender smile
And loving touch call rest awhile

God is sure. He is always there
In faithfulness and constant prayer

God is true to all He says
Ever present all the days

God is here. God never fails
He clears the mist of mourning veils

God is felt. God is known
God is closest when alone

God is found in many ways
Where there is Love is where He stays

Colours of My Heart

Blue reminds me I belong to Mary. White I belong to God
Green of hope, peace. Red His most precious Blood

Purple His dear Passion. Dark most cruel pain
Yellow He is Risen, in Light to come again

Holy, holy, holy is the Lord God Almighty
He was, He is and He is to come. Rev.4:8

All colours of the rainbow, every colour across the land
Tell of our Creator. All comes from His mighty Hand

Holy Spirit

Holy Spirit come today
Listen Spirit as I pray
Holy Spirit show me how
You are living in me now

Holy Spirit make me bend
To the Word that You might send
Renew me Lord. Call my name
Breath of God, oh breathe again

Holy Spirit reach to me
Touch my soul so tenderly
Spread Thy wings, Holy Dove!
Fill me with Thy wondrous Love

Holy Spirit! Holy Fire!
Make Your will my one desire
Guide me Lord, let me know
In which direction I should go

Holy Spirit help me hear
Freeing me from all fear
Comforter! Save me from
Guilt that I may dwell upon

Holy Spirit make me whole
Put Your joy into my soul
Light of Lights! Drawing near
Gift of God so shiny clear

Holy Spirit bless me with
All the Love You have to give
Mighty power! God's own Self
Send Your healing, send us health

Holy Spirit bringing grace
Show the Beauty of God's Face
Lead me onward. Let me see
All God has to offer me

Teach me *Spirit*, how to live
How to love, how to forgive
How to pray, how to sing
Praising You in everything. Amen.

Though He Was God

Did You think it through, Lord
When You came to earth
Could You already see all You began
By coming down from Heaven
Leaving Heaven's wealth
To come to share
The poverty of man

Did you think it through, Lord
When the Father said
That You would leave the comfort of His side
Were You eager to obey
Or did You hesitate
To come to earth to seek
Your Heavenly bride

Did Mary think it through, Lord
How could she have known
Quite all You would accomplish as her Son
So many souls You gained
By the Virgin's loving 'Yes'
Bearing You - The Christ -
For everyone

Should we think it through, Lord
When You speak our name
O How glorious is that day we hear
The movement of Your Spirit
Calling us to come
And follow on the Way
That keeps You near

Lord, by Your example, Very God in man
How wonderful the mystery You present
Giving grace to do Your will
Showing us Your love

Present here in Word
And Sacrament

Behold the Lamb of God

O What a Saviour! Behold the Lamb of God
Who, from the Cross of Calvary imparts
Plenitude of grace
For all the human race
And comes
To heal us
At the centre of our hearts

O What a Saviour! Behold the Lamb of God
Who, through His Crown of Thorns imparts
A wreath of tenderness
And His loveliness
And comes
To heal us
At the centre of our hearts

O What a Saviour! Behold the Lamb of God
Who, through His open Side imparts
Food to feed our soul
Love to make us whole
And comes
To heal us
At the centre of our hearts

O What a Saviour! Lord of Heaven and earth
Who through His Resurrection never parts
Behold the Lamb of God
O See the way He trod
To come
To live
Within the centre of our hearts

Through His wounds you have been healed. 1 Pt.2:24

Except Through Me

Jesus said, 'I am the Way, the Truth and the Life.
No one can come to the Father except through Me.' Jn.14:6

Make a friend of the Cross, My child
It is the only way to come
To the Kingdom of God forever
With My Beloved Son

Make a friend of the Cross, My child
Life can sometimes seem unfair
But the Cross is for those who follow the Way
Ah - see who else stood there

Make a friend of the Cross, My child
It is the only way to see
Each step taken by Jesus
Is a step that leads to Me

My Son carried the Cross
And returned to Heaven above
So you receive His Spirit to know
My everlasting love

Make a friend of the Cross, My child
You know that is where I am found
Take your cross and follow My Son
Come, worship on holy ground

Come Follow Me

I want to carry on Lord, I want to do Your will
But Jesus, I am asking You to help me climb this hill

I want to carry on Lord, for You revealed the Way
Jesus, I want to follow You and pick up my cross each day

We know that You grew weary Lord. We know You are The Son
We know Yours is the Very Cross we look and lean upon

Lord, as You have called me, You will surely know
How much I want to carry on and upwards, onwards go

Lord, have You forgotten me. Can You tell me why
I cannot seem to take a step however hard I try

Lord, are You in hiding. Come, show Your lovely Face
For I continue only in Your supply of grace

Lord, come to my rescue. Let me not be put to shame
Can't You hear how very loudly I am calling on Your name

I want to carry on Lord. I want to do Your will
But Lord, I am asking You to help me climb this hill

Can You Drink This Cup?

Lord, if You can do this, so can I
You who took the Cross
And showed us how to die

You, though God, as man taught us prayer
Even when Your heart was wearied
And Your spirit sadly bare

Lord, if You can suffer who am I
To waver when I know
You hear my every cry

So I will drink the Cup You offer me
And take the path that leads
Into eternity

I'll follow on to where You took my place
And became the Source
Of God's amazing grace

We come. You give sufficient for our need
And as our Loving Shepherd
Take the lead

O Lord, be praised! Lord, who did not die in vain!
Through Your glorious Resurrection
We are born again!

*Jesus said, 'Can you drink the cup that I shall drink,
or be baptised with the baptism
with which I shall be baptised?' Mk.10:38*

Baptism - A Meeting

Like a darkened cave
The soul awaits the touch of God to remove all shadow
Or like a desert awaits the rain
To transform its appearance to that of a meadow

Like the rays of the sun
The Spirit hovers. God Himself comes to remove all sin
Coming to heal, to bless, to love
And to let His eternal light shine in

A child of God,
His truly beloved, is called on a journey and makes a start
Learning to listen, learning to pray
As the Spirit enlightens the mind and heart

Through this glorious meeting -
Baptism - God lives in us as in Christ we remain
Unfurling the way, providing the strength
With untold graces and Heaven to gain

God-is-with-us
Every step of the way, throughout our joy, throughout all sorrow
God is I AM, unchanging and true
He was and is and will be tomorrow

Through loving obedience
Of the Son, God is 'fixed' in this indelible sign
The Spirit moves and comes to rest
Finding the soul where He is pleased to shine

Delight is found
In this great mystery. God through His Spirit such power displays
Wonder abounds in the soul who believes
It is saved. Yet lost in everlasting praise

The Presence of The Lord

O to capture the feeling
Of freshness in the Spring
When everything is turning bright and new
When all the world seems right again
And days are full of hope
Floating by dressed with a golden hue

O to capture the feeling
When things are at their best
For like a bubble happiness disappears
Swiftly goes the sunny day
Swiftly comes the cloud
That turns the sweetness into a veil of tears

We don't need to capture a feeling
When the Lord is at our side
For He will turn all darkness into Light
His Presence tells us He is here
With healing power and grace
As we walk with Him and keep Him ever in sight

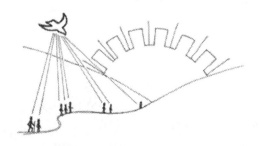

In You is the source of life; by Your light we see the light. Ps 36:9

Only Through Me

Only through You, Lord
Only then true peace
Through Your sacred Wounds will all strivings cease

Only through You comes strength
Fortitude and grace
Sufficient to withstand difficulties we face
Only in seeking we find
Only in prayer we hear
Only through Your Precious Blood know Your Presence near

Through You we are healed
Through You alone we see
How great the love You offered to us on Calvary
Through You our heart can cry
'Abba', our Father too
And receive Your Spirit. Only, my Lord, through You

Only through You we learn
Which way to journey on
Through Your Cross You show how God's will is done

Lord, had You not suffered
We could not come to know
The power of Your wounds and mercy You bestow
Through Your loving sacrifice
The soul can know its rest
Your Majesty shines forth and all the world is blest

How Can This Be Happening

Father, are You listening. Can You hear my prayer
I thought You'd sent Your only Son so I could know His care

O Jesus can You really hear. Have You turned away Your Face
How can this be happening. I'm lost without Your grace

Perhaps you have forgotten
Have you not understood
The meaning of My Cross
And the power of My Blood

Yes, Lord. But what is happening. Just show another way
Point in a direction that will prove a brighter day

Ah! I see you have forgotten
Things that happened on the Hill
How the Son surrendered
To the Father's perfect will

You only have to contemplate
What happened there to Me
This should help you carry
Your cross more easily

Yes Lord. I hear Your words. I know that they are true
But it seems wherever I may search my gaze can't fix on You

Come, let My Holy Spirit
Turn you round to see
How very great My love for you
But child, do you love Me?

Behold the Wonders I Perform!

Be magnified Lord in our lives
Let us spread Your Gospel Word anew
Nothing else can cause mankind
To hunger and believe
Nothing else and no one Lord, but You

Be magnified Lord in this age
Help us live our lives as You desire
Give the gifts we need today
Come, renew the earth
Setting it ablaze with holy fire

Be magnified Lord once again
Let Your Spirit move around the earth
Gathering from pole to pole
The elderly, the young
Bringing all Your people to new birth

Be magnified Lord in the Church
Magnified again throughout this land
Magnified in peoples' lives
Magnified in souls
That walk towards the future You have planned

Be magnified throughout the world
Let all thoughts and hearts beat the same
To see beyond the wonders
Man himself achieved
And feel the power in Your holy name

Praise the name of Jesus

Gethsemane

I don't want to go to sleep Lord
I want to stay awake
This garden is so gloomy
but I'll do this for Your sake

I'll be here when they come for You
How could I fall asleep
When Your hour is approaching
With You, this watch I'll keep

I'll be alert. I'll stay awake
I'll kneel with You in prayer
I'll not let them capture You
nor take You anywhere

But Lord, I am tired
I'll just rest beneath this tree
I'll stay awake for if I slept
what would You think of me!

I'll sit awhile and ponder days
You chose us - even me!
And how You walked on water
and calmed the storm on Galilee

You taught us ways we could never know
without our Master's hand
Miracles! You raised the dead
and made the fallen stand

You had all us enraptured by
the things You did and said
Promising eternal life –
though first we must be dead

The way You fed the thousands
on the hill that afternoon
Brought wonder in spite fears
that occasionally loom

You captivated with one look
the crowds who turned You
Oh what a Leader to follow!
You know we'll ever be true

Just call and we will run
to assist You at Your side
We want no place to lay our heads
We want no place to hide

We'll follow our Master fervently
never to turn away
Recall high on the mountain
words we heard Your Father say

You shared with us Your Father's love
Made us His children too
Things that seem impossible
are gladly done by You

You fill our minds and hearts and souls
You make us all feel new
You give us signs and wonders
We give our hearts to You

Nothing could come between us Lord
Neither wealth nor power
So I'll stay awake with You
at Your approaching hour

Ah! You know how much I love You Lord
I'm dreaming dreams so deep
In this gloomiest of gardens,
just wake me if I sleep

Nothing Has Changed

Nothing has changed
But something has moved
Deep within my soul
I know, Lord, You are healing me
And making me more whole

Nothing is new
But something has moved
Deep within my heart
I know, Lord, You are calling me
To try to make a start

Nothing is great
But something has moved
Deep within my mind
I know, Lord, You are telling me
To leave the past behind

Nothing is clear
But something has moved
Deep within my self
I know, Lord, You are giving me
Riches beyond wealth

Your Spirit moved
Everything changed
Within that hiding place
Where You, O Lord, renew me with
The wonder of Your grace

The Rugged Cross

The rugged Cross high on a Hill, behold that dreadful sight
Is calling me and beckoning to stay here through this 'night'

Hidden graces still lie there. Such is its appeal
Drawing and beckoning, despite the way I feel

The rugged Cross high on that Hill is where we meet the Lord
He longs to give to the soul unimaginable reward

The rugged Cross standing high, bids all to come to see
Drawing and beckoning to share Christ's Victory

Who can ignore that rugged Cross
Where Jesus Christ redeems
The Lord calls us to come to Him
And taste His Living streams

That rugged Cross! Can I refuse
Its wondrous hold on me
When calling and offering
Power to set me free

For on that Cross once lay the Lord
Behold that dreadful sight
He is Risen now, still beckoning
To follow in His Light

The Father gave the perfect Gift
From within His treasure store
His only Son upon the Cross
The Way to Heaven's Door

Beneath the Cross

Beneath the Cross I meet Your mother's eyes
With love she points, 'This way to Paradise'

With fear, yet joy I meet Your mother's gaze
'Child, I am here', so tenderly she says

And so I stand where Your blest mother stood
And see Your flesh with wounds that caused the blood

She kindly calls and joins her tears to mine
Our eyes behold Your Countenance divine

O Son of God. Poor words can 'nere express
I bend my knee and Thee as Lord confess

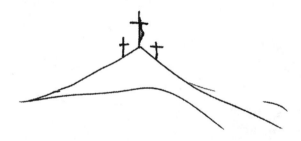

Beneath the Cross, O holy Lamb of God
Your mother calls, 'Come, follow where He trod.'

Hid in Thine Earthly Home

If you love someone you long to be near them
If you love someone you seek the time
To be near to them, to be in their presence
Your happiness is in seeing them shine

If you know someone thinks the world of you
And if that someone seeks the time
To be near to you, to be in your presence
You heart would cry out 'I'm glad you are mine'

~~~~~~~

Yet I know Someone who left His Kingdom
He suffered for me. He died on the Wood
He found the way to remain with me
In His own Body and Precious Blood

We come to His House to offer Him praise
And echo the angels around His throne
We come to adore, to take and receive
Rejoicing as people He made His own

This Royal Someone heals the sick
He raised the dead. Changed water to wine
And yet He welcomes me into His Presence
Such a Great King is a Friend of mine

And as I pray He listens to me
And carefully hears my thoughts pour out
He knows how I love to be in His Presence
And scatters His light, all within, all without

If you love someone you long to know them
If you love someone you seek the time
To be near to them, to be in their presence
And so it is with our Lord Divine

Godhead here in hiding, whom I do adore,
masked by these bare shadows, shape and nothing more.
(St. Thomas Aquinas)

You Are The Body

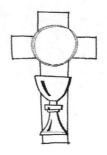

Behold the Lamb of God

You are the Body broken. You are the Word spoken
You are the Bread we eat. You are the One we meet

You give Your blood as wine. You give Yourself Divine
You are these things to me with eyes You give to see

You are the future bright. You are Eternal Light
You are the Victory. You are these things to me

You give Your Mother blest who brings our souls to rest
Within Your precious Blood and keeps us safe for God

Lord Feed Me

Lord feed my body and feed my soul
Feed my mind and make me whole
Heal me Lord, through and through
That I become more like You

Always

Always
through Your mercy, my Lord
You let us feel the sharpness of Your sword

Always through Your grace, my God
You draw us in the footsteps that You trod

Always through Your Word, my Christ
You penetrate the dark and give Light

Always through Your Love, my Jesus
You comfort us in sorrow and heal us

Always through Your Spirit whom You give
Comes holiness and power in which to live

Always through Your blessing anew
Your Flame is caused to dance, just for You

Always You are there, I am here
Always I feel Your Presence near

Always is for ever, my Lord
Ever be acknowledged and adored

Always through Your mercy alone
Always in the soul You call Your own

'I am the Alpha and the Omega'

Beyond the Cross

Beyond the Cross such glory is
This yours and mine, the pain was His

Eternal life for you and me
By His dear Blood that marked the Tree

For by His wounds and gaping side
Is Heaven's gate flung open wide

A gift of love much more than gold
O eyes of faith this Lord behold

Who from the Cross His mercy poured
Be ever praised, by all adored

Beyond the Cross life wondrous
Through His dear Blood shed for us

Everything is Mystery

Everything is mystery but when the Lord appears
He lifts the mystic veil undoing doubt and fears

He reveals His Majesty, the power of His grace
Burning passion reigns at the showing of His Face

Beautiful captivity! To never be the same
Held fast within His love. O Glorious His name!

The Lord the Most High is glorious,
the great King over all the earth. Ps.47:2

The True Light

Like a star in the night is our Risen Lord
In splendour, radiant and fair
His brightness conquers everything
Shedding Light around
The Light that gently says 'God is there'

Long ago, high above, was the Eternal Word
The Son, already shining bright
The Father saw a hungry world
Lacking faith and love
And silently He sent His 'True Light'

'Twas a star in the night that led mankind to see
Our Saviour, with birth so very dear
The Same undimmed upon the Hill
Whom death could not conceal
The Light that gently says 'God is here'

Like a star in the night, yet on our altars now
Is Jesus, Lamb of Calvary
Giving us God's holy Gift
Present for all time
The Light that gently says 'This is Me'

The Christmas Gift

A child was born. God was He
Who made the stars. Yet maketh me

His blood was rich. With saving power
Who conquered death. And Satan's hour

Eternal life with Him above
His gift to me Whose name was Love

For a son has been born for us, a son has been given to us,
and dominion has been laid on his shoulders;
and this is the name he has been given:
'Wonder-Counsellor, Mighty-God,
Eternal-Father, Prince-of-Peace'. Is.9-5

God Awakes

God awakes with a call none but His lovers hear
Gentle whispers showing how the Lord is ever near

God awakes with a sigh, deep, deep as deep can be
Wanting. Drawing, showing how He died for love of me

God awakes with a touch telling He is real
Moving. Showing how His power can wonderfully heal

Praise to God, Father, Son, praise the peaceful Dove
Glory, honour, blessing, might, to Him who reigns above

God awakes with such Love none but His own receive
Willing. Calling. Showing how to follow and believe

Thank You Lord

Thank You Lord, for all You give
Within this heart of mine
The place where You are living
Your Holy Spirit's shrine

Thank You Lord, for who You are
The Beginning and the End
Mighty God! Good Shepherd
My Saviour. My Friend

Thank You Lord, that when You come
Again on shining train
All evil will be banished
And only joy will reign

Thank You Lord, caring now
For all humanity
Watching over everyone
Yet living, Lord, in me

Because of Mary's 'Yes'

The Virgin will conceive and give birth to a son
whom they will call Immanuel, a name which means 'God-is-with-us'. Mt.1:23

The world is so rich
Because of Mary's 'Yes'
She bore God's only Son
To reconcile and bless

The Word is made Flesh
Because a maiden said
'Let what You have said be done
Let all the world be fed'

Not with manna now
But by Heavenly decree
Our Saviour came to say
'This Flesh and Blood is Me'

Jesus gave Himself!
And His enlightened ones
Call His Father 'Abba'
Beloved daughters, sons

The world would be dark
Like people with no sight
Walking in the gloom
Without His glorious Light

His birth gave new Life
More than the world could guess
God's Kingdom comes to reign
Because of Mary's 'Yes'

God Is Love

God is Love
There is no other reason
Love alone
Is why God sent His Son
Love alone
Can answer any question
And like an endless river
Ever run

Love remains
When everything is dying
Love remains
When others go away
Love remains
When promises are broken
Love alone supports us
On our way

God is Love
In this is found the meaning
God remains
When all else moves away
God alone
Gives in such abundance
God is Love. Giving Love
Each day

A Light in the Dark

I'm a candle, a light for God
With a wick running straight through my heart
He can melt me and use me and form me until
I'm completely His work of art

I'm a candle, a light for God
With a wick running straight through my heart
He can cut me and burn me and shape me until
All shades of darkness depart

Be a candle, a light for God
With His love running straight through your heart
Let Him shine, let Him glow, till others can see
He has called you and set you apart

Be a candle, a shining light
That nothing at all could snuff out
Let no storm, no gloom, nor thunderous clouds
Make you stumble or cause you to doubt

Receive this Light

Be a candle, a light for God
Let Him set you afire to melt
Let Him live. Let Him reign. Let Him purify
Till love conquers all it is dealt

Life

Life is for living in Christ each day
In light, in darkness, He is the Way

Life is a mixture, of faith, of doubt
That makes a soul sing and hearts cry out

Life turns a corner, God's mercy is great
Knowing in sorrow such joys await

His gifts come with grace and Wisdom to guide
Knowing our Saviour at our side

His ways are unseen but, like a breath
He flows through our hearts. In life. In death

Life is uncertain, nothing is sure
Except that Jesus holds every cure

He offers nothing that is not good
He took evil's ways upon the Wood

Life is fragile yet firm and strong
Secured in The Christ to whom we belong

Life is given. Or taken away
On earth tomorrow. In Heaven today

Life is a blessing. Life passes swift
Life is from God. Life is His gift

Lord, I'm Frazzled

Lord, I'm frazzled. It's been a long day
And I can't make sense of the things people say

They speak of a world where You don't reside
Due to fears they hold deep inside

They talk of all things, all points of view
They chatter along but they won't mention You

It leaves my mind empty, longing to hear
That Voice within telling You're near

How blessed are we who know we can come
And enter Your rest as Thy will is done

And so I am praying, dear Lord, once again
Thy Kingdom come. Come Lord, come reign

Reign in all hearts so precious to You
Seen as our Father, living and true

Maranatha

Come, Lord, come

When I Am Gone

When I am gone
And leave this flesh behind, weep not for me
Rejoice! For I have gone to live with God
Eternally

One thing I ask. My final wish
Remember
To love. Be kind. Be good
Be compassionate and tender

Days pass as quickly as the turning of the tide. The secret is
To be thankful as you store a host of golden memories

Ones that speak of challenges, victories and yes, some pain
Hold them close with gentle thoughts that linger till the day we meet again

Can you imagine a place where no one cries. I am here
God Himself has taken all my hurts and wiped away my every tear

The shell in which I grew is aged now. Its end has come
It grew tired and so weary and wanted Heaven as my Home

Now I am gone
I leave this flesh behind. Weep not for me
It is done. My Father's House is where I shall live
Eternally

With Him I'll live in harmony for ever more
It is done. I've simply gone through death and entered Heaven's door

From here I'll keep watch over you, with angels, night and day
But now and then, pause awhile. Remember me, and pray

He will wipe away all tears from their eyes;
there will be no more death,
and no more mourning or sadness. Rev.21:4

A Priest's Daily Prayer

I used to watch another
bringing down the Son -
the Flesh to eat, the Blood to drink - food for everyone

Today I see another
bring this Bread to earth -
the Flesh to eat, the Blood to drink - God and man at birth

I now am the other
I, who bring this Feast -
the Flesh to eat, the Blood to drink. I, who am the priest

Mary guard my prayer
enliken me to Him -
The Alpha and the Omega - Holy, free from sin

Jesus let me always see
bringing You, the Lamb -
The Word made Flesh, the Risen Lord - who and what I am

I, who am Your servant
called to bring this Feast -
the Flesh to eat, the Blood to drink - Your consecrated priest

Who Gave the First Heart Breath

Who gave the first heart breath. Who displayed His might
Who created the sun for day, the moon with stars for night

Who gave the first heart breath. Who gave the first flower seed
Whose Spirit hovered over earth and made it 'good indeed'

Order came from chaos. Purpose to each thing
Each tree with its own fruit to bear. Each bird its song to sing

Whose power made this world. Such miracles for us
Unparalleled in Beauty. From void and space and dust

Who gave the first heart breath, then, in His Master plan
Gave Jesus to each loving soul – Who but the great 'I AM'

He made the first heart beat. He brought all things to 'be'
His power made this Universe. Yet moves in you and me

He is the God of all, the unseen and the seen
He sends His Paraclete to show all that His wonders mean

A mystery so deep, no words can e're explain
But gifts of faith and hope and love adore His holy Name

Praise to the Holy Spirit. Praise to the Holy Son
All praise to our Creator, Father of everyone. Amen

In These Days

It is easy with hindsight to see
How God wants His will to be done
How He through the ages prepared
The way for His beloved Son

In past days God spoke through His prophets
Those He favoured, His appointed ones
All the time longing to make us
His adopted daughters and sons

When the people of Israel wandered
God led them by His own hand
Through the prophets and signs and wonders
He spoke of the Promised Land

God carefully prompted and guided
In the desert and right through the sea
Gathering, calling, providing
Revealing the place they should be

God so loved His people Israel
Out of Jesse would spring the One
To lead all people from darkness
Shining more brightly than the sun

Today God gives us vision to see
As we listen to Him each day
In answer to Jesus and follow
The Life, the Truth and the Way

In these days God pours out His Spirit
In trust His children remain
Waiting in joyful hope
Of our Saviour coming again

Drink My Everlasting Water

Drink My everlasting water. I always can supply
For My real life is endless. I never can run dry

It is God who comes to offer this water without end
If you but come to meet Him such healing He will send

Drink My eternal waters. Not from the soil it springs
But from within where it may seem your soul is given wings

Come, journey with My Spirit
Come, walk the way I show
Come to Me, My lovely one
Come, God your Father know

He waits for you to taste
The water found in Me
Glad to be found in finding
Delighting equally

The Spirit comes imparting life
No other power can tell
Come to Me, all who thirst
I am the Living well

The Father gave His Son
And still He gladly gives
The waters flowing freely
To show that Jesus lives

Jesus said, 'Whoever drinks this water will get thirsty again;
but anyone who drinks the water that I shall give
will never be thirsty again.' Jn.4:14

Our God

The Spirit can enter that darkest of places
Where we've known fear and dread
The Spirit can take all hurting away to leave His Peace instead

The Spirit can enter the darkest of minds
And bring His Light to shine
Where crevices, however dark, can be filled with truth Divine

The Spirit can enter the saddened heart
However sore it feels
Flowing through its passages, miraculously He heals

The Spirit can enter the hardened soul
Frozen, cold as the grave
His tender warmth prising apart, to sanctify and save

The Spirit can enter wherever He wills
Our muscles, our sinews, our flesh
Our mind, our heart, our body, our soul, with power to refresh

This is our God, the Father, the Son
The Spirit who brings such grace
Caring, moulding, healing until, we are forever face to Face

The Spirit can enter our deepest point
Of suffering and pain
If only we invite Him in. Invite Him in, to reign

Veni Sancte Spiritus Veni Sancte Spiritus Veni Sancte Spiritus

The Paraclete

Whatever time of the morning, whatever time of the day
Whatever time of the afternoon
He is with us here to stay

Whatever time in the evening, whatever time of the night
He is with us throughout all darkness
Our ever shining Light

He is with us when things are difficult. He is with us when we mourn
He gently wipes a tear away
And carries over the storm

He is with us as we laugh and sing, He is ever at our side
He accompanies us at all times
And gently turns the tide

This was one of His promises, this comfort ours to know
Though Jesus ascended to Heaven
He remains with us here below

O thank the Lord for everything. His mercy shows what is best
So thank the Lord for everything
Even things we see as a test

He is with us throughout our journey, whether its night or day
Our Lord who keeps His promises
Is with us here to stay

Jesus said, 'Know that I am with you always; yes, to the end of time.'
Mt.28:20

This Journey

This journey is like no other we will ever undertake
For we travel all the further without baggage we might take

This journey is eternal. Its resting found at death
Our final destination arrives with our last breath

It starts within the womb. God watches us with care
Breathing life into the soul He lovingly placed there

We need the Holy Spirit to help us move along
To be our inspiration and fill us with His song

We need an open heart with love filled to the brim
Handing Him the only key to show our trust in Him

We need a searching mind to know God's holy Word
Guided by the surest route that ever can be heard

We need to stop for prayer to help us see the way
And learn to read the signposts still calling, come what may

He leads us over hill and dale though with no path to see
He lightens up His footprints to glow sufficiently

We need no map or compass. We need none of those things
For then God can carry us upon His angels' wings

And take us to our Homeland still there to be our Friend
In a land with no beginning, a place without an end

O Father, May We Be One

O Father, may we be one
As Jesus intended for us
When He gave Himself and died
So dreadfully on the Cross

O Father, let us all see
Not our way, but Yours, O Lord
Seeing everything Jesus meant
Through His heart pierced by that sword

O Father may we all turn
To look upon Calvary
To see again those dreadful wounds
That made us children of Thee

Let Your will be done, not ours
Through the suffering of Your Son
Unite our hearts more deeply
By His blood that made us one

He came not to divide
But to lead us the same way
Through the power of the Holy Spirit
To one God, one Father, we pray

Trust In God

Such a long way to go. Such a long way to travel
Through the complexities of life
As God's Word and His ways
Unravel

Sometimes life seems easy. Sometimes this journey seems hard
But Jesus is our inspiration
With His angels around
To guard

Maybe a long way to go, though such a distance behind
As the mysteries of God unfurl
And the hills and valleys
Unwind

God knows how long to go. Each day we need to decide
To be ready in but an instant
Should He call us
Eternally
To His side

Good Shepherd

The Lord has provided rest for me
Upon this journeys way
That room within where I find Him
Whenever I stop and pray

The Lord has provided strength for me
Where deep within my soul
He pours His sacramental grace
Renewing. Making whole

The Lord has provided for all our needs
Through His sanctifying power
In readiness for He may come
At unexpected hour

The Lord has provided all manner of things
Through the Cross of Christ our Lord
He gives His Kingdom to our hearts
And Heaven as reward

For the Lord sent His Almighty Word
That leapt from up on high
All people who believe in Him
Shall live and shall not die

The Lord has provided a home for me
When journeying is done
He will place the Crown of Life on my head
The race faithfully won

Turn To Me and Be Saved

Son of God made flesh what have we done to You
Is my sin among those which scarred Your body
Show me Lord, teach me through Your wounds
that I may be cleansed though mortified
healed though first torn apart

Son of God. Made flesh for me
Son who bore our sin be with this broken world
Show us in this day and age how to love one another
through despair, through anger, through hurt
through insecurity, indignation, infidelity, blindness

Teach us how to love as You loved upon the Cross
when You forgave those who nailed You to the Tree
and let You hang so heavy, and die
that we might see what real love is

Let us love with Your compassion

What is love
if it bears no trace of that You showed on Calvary

Love is joy and laughter and fun and care-free hours
But love is also pain when misunderstandings show their head
and dark silences appear and confusion grows and spreads
when rejection is around
and lies are told instead of truth
and persecution fills the air
O Lord, who alone are Truth and Beauty
grant us grace to be open to that love
uniting us to You, our heart to Yours
a child to Father. The Father to His child

Let our eyes be fixed on You, like a servant to her Master
so that we may serve the world in peace and justice and truth
You are the Son who came to save this world
the Precious One who obeyed His Father's will
Lord, who washed the feet of Your disciples
teach us humility

Lord who gave Your very Flesh and Blood, help us share
Help us give our time that others might know
we care enough to give that which can never come again
Help us share our needs as well as our gifts
Help us be Your sisters and Your brothers in this world

Lord, King at birth
yet from the stable to the Cross You lived in need
Teach us that nakedness of spirit that attaches us to The Father
making us His daughters, His sons, through His only Beloved

What can turn the world about to You, O Lord
What can awaken the selfish heart
to even share his bread with hungry man
Yet if our tears could fill a reservoir, our fast fill a void
mans' true thirst, mans' true hunger
could only be ever truly satisfied by You

Let our repentance reveal Your anguish
Let our sorrow reveal Your grief
You came. You died. You rose to give each person a heart of flesh

Where is it found but at the Cross

Turn all eyes to You, O Lord
Draw all mankind again along the path on which You walked
And when his eyes
fall on Yours, turn him yet again
to meet that need in fellow man

Who can change the world but You, O Lord
and one surrendered to the work of Your Cross

On Calvary love forgives
Your Waters flow
O Son of God where You want change
begin with me

O Holy Mary

O Holy Mary, full of grace, with loving obedience
you did answer God with such an open heart
it should make all man shudder to see his own so closed

Mary, full of grace becoming Virgin-Mother
from your spotless womb you grew the secret of salvation
What trust you held in God
We now know the Easter Day
and how the Cross was finished but that was all unknown for you
What mystery. What love of God and willingness
Mary, simple Mother of a human child born within a place
bereft of warmth and wealth and riches
and all things telling that within your arms you held God
With silence and acceptance you took each day upon a hidden path -
the lonely one leading to the Cross
You did not doubt for you yourself had borne this Child from Heaven
conceived in you by the power of God's Holy Spirit

When love is great enough to save the world it must be one
United though apart. Joined as by a thread of Light from Him
whose unseen power is mightier than all suffering and sorrow
And Love is faithful to the end, steadfast in its sight
and true beyond its reason

O Holy Mary, full of grace, asked by God
to give His very Son to us, make me His disciple
As you were lifted up to Heaven raise my thoughts
As you were crowned with glory win my mind
As you were called to enter God and Him in you, fit me for your Son

May the arms that cradled Him carry me
May the hands that guided Him care for me
May the love you showed to God dwell in me
May the life that moved in you breathe in me

O Holy Mary, blessed, and full of grace
united in the Heavens with your Son
honoured by the Lord for bearing Him,
pray for me. Amen

Stay Close to Our Lady

To stay close to Our Lady is to stay close to Our Lord
To walk where Jesus is Ever-adored

Where He is the centre of worship and praise
Where His name is honoured throughout all days

Where His way is Life. And each word He said
Is the Truth that lasts by Whom souls are fed

To be near Our Lady is to please The One
Who chose this handmaid to bear His Son

In a world with a will of its own accord
To be near our Mother is to follow the Lord

For she did not waver. Faithful to Him
Who kept her in grace. And without sin

She the disciple who followed her Son
Created for Him. God's favoured one

How Mary pondered the Child as He grew
The Father's will. And the things she knew

To stay close to Mary is to stay close to God
Surrendered in faith to go where she trod

There gathered into the Saviour's way
Led by the Spirit each new day

Willing to travel the steepest climb
Behold Sacred wounds. And Face divine

Lo! Jesus ascended. And drew to His side
His Virgin mother from where she can guide

The secrets of Heaven Mary knows well
The mystery of God she longs to tell

To be close to this Mother reveals God's ways
Held lovingly under His constant gaze

Giving all praise to God, Three-in-One
Close to Our Lady. Close to her Son. Amen

All Nations

Lord, send us Your Spirit
Lord, send us Your grace
Lord send sufficient for the whole human race

Lord, send Your angels
To keep us for You
Send purest waters cleansing anew

Lord bless every moment
That makes up each hour
Touching all lives with Your healing power

Bless all our families
Bless all our friends
Giving the Life that never ends

Bless all Your people
May we harmonize
With mountains, streams, the moon, sun and skies

Let us fall into
Your loving plan
The one in Your mind from before time began

Make nations willing
To seek a new start
Lord, turn us again to look into Your heart

Lord, let us fall into Your loving plan

I Am Going to Heaven

I am going to Heaven
The Lord has told me so
Of all the knowledge in the world
This I want to know

I am going to Heaven
The Lord invited me
Of all the places I could choose
This is where I want to be

I'll make my way towards Him
And hear what He might say
As I continue joyfully
Along my Saviour's way

All beauty that is around us
All wealth upon this earth
Compete not with His matchless love
And promise of rebirth

He has won me Heaven
Through His grace alone
Following Him who called me
I'll worship round His throne

Meantime, full of courage
With faith strong and bold
I gladly offer service
To my God Whom I behold

My eyes will ever look to see
My ears will ever strain
My heart will stand in readiness
Till that Day He comes again

For all the wounds He suffered
For all His blood outpoured
For all His tender love to me
I gladly call Him Lord

I am going to Heaven
Ransomed and redeemed
Because I put my trust in Him
On Him my soul has leaned

Waiting On The Lord

Lord are You listening
Let not our hearts be vexed
As You prepare us for
What is to happen next

Lord, let us see Your will for us
Help us see Your Light
Never separated from
The Beauty of Your sight

Lord, whichever way we turn
Let it be following You
There is no other path to tread
But that You lead us through

Be our comfort and our guide
In Your Presence silent, still
There is no other way to seek
And find Your holy will

There is no other way to walk
O Lord as life unfolds
Waiting as You prepare us
For all the future holds

Printed in the United States
By Bookmasters